BILL WANNAN SELECTS

Stage-coach Stories of Old Australia

A BOX-SEAT MISCELLANY

Sun Books · Melbourne

Sun Books Pty Ltd
South Melbourne, Victoria 3205, Australia

First published in Australia by Sun Books 1978
This selection © Bill Wannan 1978

National Library of Australia
cataloguing in publication data

Bill Wannan selects stagecoach stories of old
    Australia

    Simultaneously published, South Melbourne, Vic.:
    Macmillan
    ISBN 0 7251 0298 5

    1. Short stories, Australian. 2. Coaching –
    Australia. I. Wannan, William Fielding, 1915–,
    comp.

A823.01

Set in Monophoto Baskerville by
The Macmillan Company of India Ltd, Bangalore
Printed in Hong Kong

BILL WANNAN SELECTS
Stage-coach Stories of Old Australia

Fire lighted; on the table a meal for sleepy men;
A lantern in the stable; a jingle now and then;
The mail-coach looming darkly by light of moon and star;
The growl of sleepy voices; a candle in the bar;
A stumble in the passage of folk with wits abroad;
A swear-word from a bedroom—the shout of 'All aboard!'
'Tchk-tchk! Git-up!' 'Hold fast, there!' and down the range we go;
Five hundred miles of scattered camps will watch for Cobb and Co.

Henry Lawson: 'The Lights of Cobb and Co.'

Editor's Note

My purpose in compiling this 'box-seat miscellany' is to take the reader on a rugged, eventful, interesting and entertaining drive into the past—into the exciting world of Cobb & Co., and the other Australian coaching lines that were brought into existence by the great gold discoveries of the early 1850s.

Like the river steamboats, the stage-coaches were ultimately put out of business, after some seventy years of vigorous life, by the railways: the long iron roads which they had helped to bring into being.

My anthology is, as far as I can make it so, a representative blend of true narrative, anecdotage, and fiction. I am indebted to the writers, living and dead, from whose work I have borrowed the reminiscences, tales, yarns and verses that follow.

I am indebted to Mr Louis A. Lothian, and the Lothian Publishing Co., of Melbourne, for permission to include 'Tale of the Old Coast Road' by Marie E. J. Pitt in this anthology.

If I have inadvertently breached any copyrights I would welcome such advice from the authors or executors concerned.

Bill Wannan

Contents

From the Box Seat

It seems that back in the 1880s a Parramatta chap, who was just recovering from a nervous breakdown, was forced by certain circumstances to pay a visit to a sheep station in the Far West of New South Wales.

This meant booking a seat on the first available Cobb coach.

Hearing that the road was very rough and that his journey would necessitate night travelling, the man from Parramatta approached the driver to find out the facts.

'Don't worry,' said the driver, 'I know every stone on the road.' In spite of this assurance our man found the going just as bad as he'd been told it would be.

At last the wheel struck an exceptionally large rock, causing the Parramatta bloke to be thrown violently against the roof of the coach. Unable to stand it any longer he put his head out of the door and yelled, 'Hey, driver, I thought you told me you knew every stone on the road!'

'So I do,' the driver shouted back. 'That was one of 'em!'

*

A Rockhampton, Qld correspondent wrote to me: 'I'm reminded of a Cobb & Co. driver in my childhood days in Western Queensland.

'He was once asked by some lady passengers if he'd ever been caught in a bushfire.

' "Oh yes," he said, "I certainly 'ave."

' "And what did you do?" asked one of the ladies.

' "Well, ma'am, I put a billy full of water under the coach, tied to the back axle. Then I drove like 'ell through the fire. When I

reached the safety of the boundary gate, that water was just on
the boil, an' ready for tea!" '

*

'The event of the week, if one happened to be at the homestead,
[in the Angledool district of New South Wales] was the arrival of
Dick Stallworthy with the mail late on Saturday. Dick ran the
coach, a kind of four-wheeled buckboard, with the mails and
passengers from Collarenebri to Angledool, about seventy miles,
changing his team every twelve or fifteen miles. We ran a dozen
horses for him at the homestead which we left in the stockyard on
Saturdays. At five o'clock Dick would come swinging in with his
team of five sweating horses, stand up, throw the reins on to the
ground, give us the mail and parcels, unyoke his team, dropping
the harness on the ground, go into the stockyard with five halters
and pick out his team—some of them half-broken animals. He
would yoke them up, pick up the ribbons, and with a wave and a
crack of the whip, the plunging kicking team would be off on the
last stage—within half an hour after arrival. Dick prided himself
on being on time and, unless it was wet, would be there at five.

'He had wonderful "hands". Once coming into Collarenebri
on the box seat with him, about a mile out of town, I saw a short
woman with a child in her arms standing on a three-foot stump at
the side of the track. "There's the missis and the kid," said Dick.
With the reins in his left hand, without slackening pace, he swung
his team alongside the stump, leaned over and with his right arm
gathered his wife up on his knee, giving her a smacking kiss. It
was as pretty a piece of romantic horsemanship as ever I saw and
could not have been done half as well in Hollywood.'

From Daryl Lindsay, *The Leafy Tree* (Melbourne, 1965)

*

From an old-timer, Mr D. S. Cooper of Proserpine, Queensland,
I heard this reminiscence:

'I well remember Cobb & Co.'s coaches, having often
travelled in them in days long passed.

'One trip I remember particularly clearly. I was on the box seat travelling to a shearing shed on the Charleville-to-Blackall route. As it was getting dark I suggested to the driver that it was time to light the lamps.'

'He told me he preferred driving in the dark—he could see better, he said! Every now and again he would turn to me and say, "There ought to be a big stump in the middle of the road somewheres about here," or "I reckon we'll strike the fallen log just around the next bend."

No doubt he was only pulling my leg, but I wasn't sorry when the journey was over.'

*

And talking of Cobb coaches, I can't resist passing on this reminiscence which I found among the papers of an early Victorian pioneer.

The story, absolutely true, belongs to the late 1860s when 'the scab', a virulent and disastrous disease, was causing havoc among the sheep flocks in Western Victoria.

It was also the day of 'sheep washing', many washers being employed on some stations to guide the jumbucks through baths or soaks of water into which soda and soft soap had been dissolved.

On the occasion in question a city lady was travelling on a Cobb & Co. coach. Her fellow-passengers were two well-known Western District pastoralists.

The two men soon got into conversation, and, as was natural, the talk was of general station topics. The lady was horrified to hear the following:

'How are things with you now, John?'

'Oh, much as usual. I'm still "scabby."''

A pause, then:

'How about yourself? Do you wash at all nowadays?'

'No—as a matter of fact I haven't washed for years.'

The lady from the city, distastefully eyeing the two pioneers in their moleskins, Tasmanian blueys and cabbage-tree hats, vacated her seat at the first stopping-place and asked the driver if she could continue the journey on the box seat.

From *Australasian Post* (26 October 1961)

*

'My aunt and I went into Cloncurry, Qld by the Normanton coach, which was only a small one with five horses. Our driver was a tall, thin, elderly man with a remarkable voice—it never seemed to grow weary, no matter how much he used it. Jim the Grumbler was the name he was known by.

'Rain had started, and we could only travel at about four miles an hour. We stayed the night at a mail stage. Next day we had a late start and only managed fifteen miles by twelve o'clock, when we found that the Dargale Creek was a banker. We were forced to camp—no blankets, nothing to eat, and only a mile away on the other side of the torrent a homestead! Fortunately for us, the manager sent a black boy over with a tub and some food. It was a hard swim, but we were thankful for the bread and jam.

'After the billy had boiled and tea was over, down came the rain. The black boy was the only one who had a tent, which he gave to us; the men cut some branches over which they placed bits of bark, and we had quite a comfortable sleep.

'We ate what was left of our food for breakfast next morning, by which time the creek was crossable. Some of the men came down from the station to see the coach safely over. The water was running through the coach, and once or twice the horses could not reach the top of the bank, letting the coach run backwards, which made us very uneasy. At last we galloped up to the station in great style, and all had a cup of tea!'

From N. Miller, 'Outback Travel in the Early Days (Queensland)', in *Walkabout* (1 June 1956)

*

'Apart from bushrangers, the greatest danger came from road accidents. Brake failure on steep winding hills, a shieing horse followed by a headlong bolt, breaks in the harness; these were only a few of the causes of coaching accidents which claimed the lives of Cobb & Co. drivers.

'The following, taken from an article written in 1907 by W. G. Randall, vividly describes a hair raising experience on Tapley's Hill on the Adelaide to Willunga coach run: "Somewhere about 60 years ago there was a changing place at the top of O'Halloran Hill. A most unsuitable position. On one occasion just as the ostler released the new team, the offside leader started rearing and finally bolted, taking the whole team with him 'hell for leather' down the hill. Andy jammed the brakes hard on, to no purpose. Away we went, taking the first turn on two wheels, down Tapley's Hill the coach lurched like a Dutch galliot before a gale of wind. Every one aboard was expecting a terrific crash. By the mercy of providence a wood-carter had thoughtfully dropped a log off his load. The off fore wheel hit the obstruction fair and square. This temporary easing of the pace enabled Andy to regain control of the team and brought us to a standstill near the Flagstaff Hotel at the foot of the hill. The wheel skidded the log; had it jumped it there would have been a serious fatality. The passengers clambered down and went hot foot to the front bar, and there relieved their nervous tension."'

From Max Colwell, *Australian Transport* (Sydney, 1972)

*

'Because of the depredations of bushrangers, it had become a custom, when sending money by mail coach, to cut the bank notes in two, sending one half by one mail and the other half by a later despatch, for the banks, of course, would not honour a halved note. But this custom, designed to foil the highwaymen, made them even more active, for, to put any value on the half-notes which they obtained in one hold-up, they would have to stage further attacks in the following days, in the hope of securing the other portions of the divided currency.'

From Beresford Rea, *Up and Down the Sydney Road: The Romance of the Hume Highway* (Melbourne, 1958)

*

'The arrest of [the Victorian bushranger] Captain Melville, although it removed the central figure in . . . the third bush-ranging epoch in Australia, by no means put a stop to the crime. Melville had been a specialist, a true highwayman, while the others were merely general practitioners who were not very particular what crimes they committed so long as they secured booty. On 24 January 1853, the driver of the mail coach from Colac to Geelong [in Victoria] was ordered to bail up near Mr Dennie's station. The driver kept on. One of the bushrangers reached out to grasp the reins, while the other fired at the driver. The report frightened the horse of the man who was trying to seize the reins, and it bolted, throwing the rider, The mail-man whipped his horses into a gallop and got safely away.'

From George E. Boxall, *History of the Australian Bushrangers*
(London, 1908, 3rd edn.)

*

'In the declining years of coaching, Cobb & Co. opened a number of stores in Queensland, and employed some of their old drivers as salesmen. To men accustomed to the movement and freedom of a driver's open air life, this must have been a painful translation. There is a bush jingle which sums it up:

And now we find old Bill behind the counter, half unsexed;
He's selling hose and women's clo's,
He murmurs "And what next?"

Yes! Driver Bill, whose fame is still
Renowned from Bourke to Hay,
Now humbly stands and smoothes his hands,
"Yes, madam, step this way."

'There is little doubt, however, that when they handed over the reins to their successors, they did so with mixed feelings, perhaps uttering some half-cynical, half-wistful comment, like the words which Ned Devine, on his retirement from coaching in

New Zealand, is reported to have spoken to the man who took over from him:

"Mind the peat-bog, and give my love to the tussocks." '

From K. A. Austin, *The Lights of Cobb and Co.* (Adelaide, 1967)

*

'We made up our minds to start by Saturday's coach. It left at night and travelled nigh a hundred miles by the same hour next morning. It's more convenient for getting away than the morning. A chap has time for doing all kinds of things just as he would like; besides, a quieter time to slope than just after breakfast. The Turon daily mail was well horsed and well driven. Nightwork though it was, and the roads dangerous in places, the five big double-reflector lamps, one high up over the top of the coach in the middle with two pair more at the side, made everything plain. We Cornstalks never thought of more than the regular pair of lamps, pretty low down, too, before the Yankee came and showed us what cross-country coaching was. We never knew before. My word, they taught us a trick or two. All about riding came natural, but a heap of dodges about harness we never so much as heard of till they came to the country with the gold rush.'

From 'Rolf Boldrewood', *Robbery Under Arms* (London, 1888)

BILL WANNAN

A Chapter from History

Stage-coaches, carrying mails and passengers, did not play any prominent part in Australian transport development until the era of the great gold discoveries, commencing in 1851.

In Van Diemen's Land, where the confined land area led to closer settlement at a much earlier period than on the mainland, and where roads between the main settlements were kept in reasonably good condition by vast numbers of convict labourers, stage-coach lines were established as early as 1834. The coaches were steel-springed conveyances, based on English models of the period. The routes were from Hobart Town to Launceston, New Norfolk and Richmond. From 1838, chaise-carts, mostly designed to carry mails but also taking one or two passengers, began to ply along dirt tracks in several of the remoter Tasmanian regions.

In New South Wales, the first hackney-coach was introduced at Sydney in 1830. It ran between King's Wharf and Circular Quay. Different types of carts and other light conveyances were in use for public transport in both New South Wales and Victoria prior to 1851; but they operated only in the more settled areas, as between Sydney and Bathurst, and between Melbourne and Geelong. One such coach was the 'Tiger', established in 1850 to carry passengers between Sydney and Campbelltown. It took nearly eight hours to cover the distance of 34 miles.

The outer districts, beyond the limits of the main settlements, were too sparsely settled to warrant the introduction of coaching services. The folk who lived in these frontier regions had to walk or else travel by horseback, bullock-dray, waggon or tilted cart.

The gold-rushes of the early 1850s, first to the Turon diggings

8

in New South Wales, and then to Ballarat, Bendigo and Castlemaine in Victoria, caused a revolution in methods of public
transport. At first, the diggings were serviced by primitive
coaches, ill-fitted and not suitable for rough bush tracks. Among
these pioneer services was a line established by a publican named
James Watt, which ran from Melbourne to Ballarat. Another was
set up in competition by a hotel-keeper of Ballan, James Elijah
Cook.

In 1853 a marked change occurred in coaching transport with
the arrival in Victoria of an American, Freeman Cobb, who had
served an apprenticeship with the famous Wells Fargo organi-
zation. Cobb, in partnership with John Murray Peck, James
Scanlon and James A. Lamber, also Americans, set up the firm
officially described as the Australian Stage Company, but soon
popularly known as 'Cobb & Co.'.

The coaches which Cobb introduced were of a kind not
hitherto seen in Australia. They were Concord thorough-brace
vehicles, similar to those being made at Concord, New Hamp-
shire, for the rugged tracks of the American backwoods. They
were light, hickory-framed coaches with thin-spoked wheels. The
feature which gave them remarkable resilience and a measure of
comfort was the thorough-brace on which the coach-body rode:
two braces (springs) made of several extremely stout straps of
harness leather, the ends of which were clamped and bolted.
While ordinary steel springs were liable to snap when overloaded, the thorough-brace was almost unbreakable.

American-built at first, the Cobb coaches were eventually
made in Australia, Deniliquin, N.S.W, and Charleville, Qld,
being two of the main coach-building centres.

Cobb & Co.'s first route was from Melbourne to Sandridge
(Port Melbourne). When tests had proved the excellence of the
vehicles, Cobb opened his first goldfields route in January, 1854,
from Melbourne to Ballarat via Geelong. By 1859 his service
covered almost the whole of Victoria, wherever gold was being
found and people were settling. His line became a familiar sight,
the coaches flashing scarlet by day, and casting by night a

powerful glow from their five double-reflector lamps, two at the front on either side, and one in the middle, above the box seat.

The number of horses varied with the particular vehicle and route, but teams ranged from two to eight. The average speed of the vehicles was 10 m.p.h. Regularity, punctuality and courtesy were the main features that the firm built its reputation upon.

The first Cobb drivers were brought out from America. Tough men, moustachioed dare-devils in wideawake hats and buckskin breeches, smoking huge cigars, they seemed to be afraid of nothing. Floods, bushfires, the assaults of bushrangers – they took them all in their stride. The language with which they urged on their horses was a jargon of their own. They delighted and amazed their Australian passengers.

Freeman Cobb sold out his interest in the company after a few years, but his name continued to be associated with the firm's coaches until it closed down. Cobb was succeeded by another energetic American, James Rutherford, who spread a vast network of lines through New South Wales (from 1860) and Queensland (from 1865).

Australian drivers were trained, and these proved no less competent, cool-headed and polite than the Yankees. Among the Australian drivers, none earned greater fame and respect than 'Cabbage-tree Ned' Devine (1833–1909), who at one time drove the 'Leviathan' coach which plied between Ballarat and Geelong from the early 1860s. It carried nearly 100 passengers, of whom about thirty sat outside. There were separate compartments for ladies and gentlemen. Eight horses drew this outsize vehicle. Ned Devine, incidentally, earned his sobriquet from his habit of wearing a large cabbage-tree hat. Other Australian drivers well known in their day were 'Bendigo Ike' and Jim Redfearn.

By the 1870s, Cobb's company was harnessing 6,000 horses a day, and the coaches were travelling 38,000 miles a week across the face of eastern Australia. Big mail monopoly grants from the colonial governments amounted to some £95,000 a year, helping to offset the drivers' wages which annually exceeded £100,000.

The early Cobb drivers earned from £10 to £14 a week, and were given free meals and accommodation while on the job. A good driver could earn up to £1,000 a year. Grooms and postilions were paid at the rate of £4. 10s. per week.

Staging stops varied from wayside inns in the more settled parts to bark-hut and sapling-yard staging camps in the far outback. While the horses were being changed, refreshments were supplied at a low charge to the passengers. Stages were, as a rule, up to 30 miles apart, and their standards of comfort and cleanliness depended on the part of the country being traversed. While travelling, passengers spent much of their time playing cards, singing or yarning. In times of flood, the male passengers were expected to help to extricate a bogged vehicle; and there were frequent occasions in rugged country when all the passengers had to walk. Cobb & Co., and most other lines, had only one class.

Many other coaching firms sprang up in opposition to Cobb & Co. Nowland's five-horse coaches ran from Walgett in north-western New South Wales to Sydney during the 1870s. Another line in those parts was Osborne's Van Company. Irvine was among those who operated in the Gulgong and Hill End goldfields area of New South Wales. In Victoria, Ryland J. Howard had coaches running from Melbourne to Castlemaine and Bendigo from as early as 1853. In 1855, the 'People's Line of Coaches' owned by Thomas Davies, ran between Ballarat and Melbourne. In the 1880s, Sidney Kidman, later to be known as 'The Cattle King', joined forces with his brother Charlie and a bushman named Nicholas to operate a coaching service from Hungerford down to Wentworth, right through the dry back-country of western New South Wales.

Stage-coaching services were, by and large, built on gold discoveries, and followed wherever the rushes were. This applied to much of Western Australia, in the golden era of the late 19th century.

By the early 1890s coaches were plying in every part of the country where people were, from Hobart to the Gulf of Carpentaria and from Townsville in Queensland to Albany in the far West. But they were unable to compete, in the long run, with the railways, which also spread across the continent with amazing speed in the same period.

One by one the coaching firms disappeared, until only Cobb & Co. remained, and its routes were confined to regions well off the beaten track. Cobb's last coach line, between Yeulba [now called Yuleba] and Surat in Queensland, was closed down in 1924.

WILLIAM KELLY
'The Bay of Biscay'

From Life in Victoria, or Victoria in 1853, and Victoria in 1858
(London and Melbourne, 1860).

Beyond Benalla we got into a district called the Bay of Biscay,
from its excessive roughness, being one unvarying succession of
deep crab-holes, bearing a remarkable resemblance to a monster
tan-yard sometime in disuse, with the pits partially fallen in; and
I can honestly declare that I would infinitely prefer riding out a
gale in the original bay to riding over the same ground again in a
wheeled conveyance. Every now and then, after a heavy plunge
or lurch, the coachman curtly called out, 'All a-board?' by way of
inquiring if any passengers had been ejected, appearing all the
time to derive a malicious satisfaction from the groans and
ejaculations of his bruised and bewildered fellow-travellers. As
soon as it was safe to make use of the tongue, I rashly supposed
that a special paragraph in his daily orisons supplicated the
speedy introduction of improved highways, but to my utter
astonishment he solemnly declared, and I believe with unfeigned
sincerity, 'that when the roads came to be 'cadamised on the line,
he would resign his employment and go a prospecting for another
rough-and-tumble drive.' 'Why, lor' bless your innocent genius,
sir,' said he, 'if I was to set to work on them ere turnpike tracks I
would die right off o' melancholy, or become a drivin' sombulist,
for want of ikcitement to keep me awake. I'd rather drive for my
bare tucker through the Bush, than take my twelve guineas a
week into the bargain an' drive on them darned 'cadamised
awenues, with their eternal milestones, which is enough in

themselves to make a smart man stupid, for want of something to think or calculate about. I reckons my time an' distance by my own inwention – three miles and a half from the Dead Brindled Bullock to the Leaning Gum-tree, two three-quarters from that to Broken Waggon, an' four from that into Wangaratta, an' when these marks are used up, it wakes up the brain agin to inwent new ones; but them gravel-walks an' milestones are enough to make a shicer of any man.' A species of Bush reasoning against modern innovation as amusing as it is original.

ALFRED T. CHANDLER

Catching the Coach

From A Bush Idyll and Other Poems *(Adelaide and Melbourne, 1886). This verse refers to the Victorian gold-rushes of the early 1850s; and specifically to the 'digger hunts'—organized raids by the police on the gold-fields, seeking to arrest those prospectors who were not in possession of a 'Miner's Right' or licence to dig. The diggers' detestation of the police— called 'traps' or 'Joes', the latter a reference to Lieut-Governor Charles Joseph La Trobe, the symbol of power and authority in the colony—led them to devise tricks and stratagems to hinder their work and make them appear foolish.*

———————

At Kangaroo Gully in 'Fifty-two
The rush and the scramble was reckless and rough;
'Three ounces a dish and the lead running true!'
Was whispered around concerning the stuff.

Next morning a thousand of fellows or more
Appeared for invasion along the brown rise,
Some Yankees, and Cockneys, and Cantabs of yore
And B.As from Oxford in blue-shirt disguise.

And two mornings later the Nugget saloon,
With billiards and skittles, was glaring with signs,
A blind fiddler, Jim, worried out a weak tune,
Beguiling the boys and collecting the fines.

Then tents started up like the freaks of a dream
While heaps of white pipeclay dotted the slope,

To 'Dern her—a duffer!' or 'Creme de la creme!'
That settled the verdict of languishing hope.

And bustle and jollity rang through the trees
In strange combination of húmankind traits;
With feverish searchings and gay levities
The fires of excitement were fully ablaze.

Well, three mornings after, the stringybark gums
All rustled their leaves with further surprise;
They'd seen old stagers and limey new-chums,
But here were galoots in peculiar guise:

With nondescript uniform, booted and spurred,
A fierce-looking strap on the underneath lip,
An ominous shooter, a dangling sword,
A grim leather pouch above the right hip!

And maybe a dozen came cantering so,
All clanking and jaunty—authority vain—
When down through the gully rang out the word 'Joe',
And 'Joe' was sent on with a sneering refrain.

There was hunting for 'rights', and producing the same,
Or passing them on to a paperless mate,
Or hiding in bushes or down in the claim—
Such various expedients to baffle the State.

Then 'Who put him on?'—'Twig his illigant seat!'
'Cuss me, but it's purty!'—'The thing on the horse!'
'His first dacent clothes!'—'What surprise for his feet!'
Such volleys as these were soon fired at the Force.

But duty was duty. Just then through the scrub
A digger made off—he a culprit no doubt!
'Dismount you then, Wilson!' roared Sergeant Hubbub;

'Quick! follow the rascal and ferret him out.'

The sapling cadet, with budding moustache,
Then sprang to the ground in dauntless pursuit,
And, filled up with zeal and a soldier-like dash,
He felt a true hero of saddle and boot.

The gully quick echoed with taunts that were real,
Keen chaff of defiance allied to revolt,
Such sharp wordy weapons as might have been steel
From skirmishers laughing on hillock and holt.

Away went the fugitive, spurred on by haste,
Escaping the undergrowth, leaping the logs,
Yet ne'er looking back—did he know he was chased?
Said Wilson, 'He's one of the worst of the dogs!

'Some greater misdeed must have blackened his hand;
I'll have him—promotion! Stop there, or I'll shoot!'
The other ahead didn't hear the command
But sprang on unheeding o'er dry branch and root.

The chase settled down to a heavy set-to;
They ran o'er the hill and across the clear flat;
And Wilson was chuckling—the villain he knew
Was making a bee-line for jail—Ballarat!

'I'll follow the rogue safely into the trap—
Confound him, he's speedy: I can't run him down;
But there, quite unconscious of any mishap,
I'll fix him up neatly in gay Canvas Town!'

Then over a creek where a line of sage-gums
All flourishing grew, then away to the right;
Their loud breathings mingled with strange forest hums,
And wallabies scampered with terror and fright.

And cockatoos screeched from the loftiest trees,
The minahs and magpies all fluttered and flew,
The drowsy old possums were roused from their ease,
The locusts and lizards quick stepped out of view.

But on went the pair, never noticing this,
For both had a serious business in hand.
With one there were feelings that prophesied bliss,
The other saw capture and glory so grand.

O'er hillside and creek, beyond hollow and spur,
Through brief strips of woodland, they hurried on still;
The trooper lost ground, but he wasn't a cur;
Besides, they were nearing on Bakery Hill.

Then suddenly broke on each sweltering sight
The thousand of tents in the city of gold;
And straight to the thick of them ran with delight
The chased and the chaser—what luck for the bold!

The coach was just starting for Melbourne that day
As Wilson rushed eagerly on to his man.
'I'll put you with care where you won't be so gay,'
The trooper in triumph already began.

'You've led me a dance in a lively hour's sun;
Now trip out your licence, or waltz off to jail!
What! got one? Oh, ho! Why the——did you run?'
'To post this here letter for Nell by the mail.'

JOHN ROBERT GODLEY

By Coach to the Turon

From Extracts from a Journal of a Visit to New South Wales in
1853 *(reprinted from* Fraser's Magazine *for November and December
1853); and quoted in Nancy Keesing's anthology,* Gold Fever *(Sydney,
1967).*

After we had become a little settled in Sydney I determined to go
to the diggings on the Turon. There were two ways of going. One
was to buy or hire a horse and ride, the other to take one of the
two 'coaches' which ply daily between Sydney and Bathurst. I
was told that the first would be far the most comfortable, and on
every account I should have preferred it, but that it would take
up too much time. But that objection was fatal, so I took my place
by the Bathurst 'mail coach', paying £2. 10s. for the 'box seat',
which I was especially advised to secure. It started from the post-
office at 4.30 p.m., and I met it there at the time appointed.

Seeing the front boot left open to receive the mail bags, I stood
by the wheel till they should be put in, as there was no place for
me to put my feet upon while the boot was open. The coachman
seeing me stand there called out, 'Ain't you going with us?' 'Yes,'
said I. 'Well, then, I advise you to get up somewhere, for I shall
start the moment the bags are in.' This sentence, delivered in a
tone and manner that seemed to be studiously made as insolent as
possible, was my first specimen of what I soon found was the
ordinary mode of proceeding among this class of people in this
country.

The coach was a very good omnibus, with four excellent
horses, well appointed too; and I began to think my friends had

19

misinformed me when they warned me against the mail. We drove to Parramatta, 15 miles, in two hours. The road is macadamized and in tolerable order; the country very ugly and uninteresting—a small proportion of it is still covered with forest; the greater part is divided into paddocks, with post and rail fences, with muddy water holes interspersed among them. . . . There was nothing however to distinguish the look of the road very markedly from what one might see in England, except the number of sheep, cattle, and horses which one met, driven by wild-looking stockmen in their shirts, white or blue, with broad-brimmed cabbage-tree hats (a sort of chip) long boots, and tremendous stock whips, and the wool drays, two-wheeled vehicles, drawn by from four to ten horses or bullocks, generally the latter, and carrying from one to two tons of wool in bales. The public-houses are frightfully numerous, yet it seemed to me as if we stopped at all of them, and wherever we stopped our driver took a glass of grog, and then had a few minutes' lounge and gossip, so that we had to go at a good pace when moving in order to keep our time. . . .

At Parramatta I found to my great disgust that we were to 'change coaches', as it was called, in other words to exchange our coach for a spring-cart, something like a very rough Irish 'inside car', with a driving seat that held two, and a body that professed to hold six, but was really fit only to hold four with tolerable comfort. The new 'coach' had a new driver, and I found that it is not the custom for successive drivers to be bound by each other's arrangements, so I lost my 'box seat', which had been already engaged by a Parramatta passenger. The body of the car was choked up by two large sacks of corn, and by the luggage of six passengers, so as to leave literally no room at all for their 12 legs, which of themselves were more than sufficient to fill it.

However, as we had to go *that* way and *there*, or stay behind, we, six of us, clambered into the horrible 'instrument', and lay or sat or stood upon each other in a kind of heap, which as we proceeded became more solid as it shook down, till I doubt whether a casual passerby would have discerned that it was composed of human limbs and bodies. At this point began the real sufferings of the journey, sufferings which all that I had heard but faintly enabled me to realize.

At Penrith, 12 miles further on, I again took my place on the 'box', and a fresh victim was placed 'inside'. This was an unwary move on my part; bad as was my position before, it was decidedly made worse by the change. The 'box' was a narrow bar of wood, without any back or sides, and sloping steeply backwards. Every jolt therefore of course tended to throw the wretched sitter violently into the body of the car, a tendency which he could only resist by convulsively clinging to his slippery seat with the calves of his legs. During most of the time I was sitting on the inside of my legs, the centre of gravity depending considerably behind and below the bar before mentioned.

And the jolts—what shall I call them? They were rather headlong plunges into an apparently bottomless abyss than jolts of the ordinary kind. You went down with a 'send', like a ship pitching 'bows under' in a head sea, and how the springs (for there were springs, though they were nearly blocked up) bore one, even the least, of these terrible shocks, is to me an inexplicable marvel.

The bodily suffering, also, was greatly aggravated by the other annoyances of the journey. In the first place, during the early part of the night it rained rather heavily, and a drizzling mist continued through the whole of it; then the companions I was afflicted with! I don't remember having on a journey in any other country met with habitual and wanton incivility. But here everybody you came in contact with, drivers, passengers, hostlers, chamber-maids, seemed to take a sort of pride in being rude and insolent, so that by degrees I became really almost afraid to address the slightest observation to any one, as it was pretty sure to produce an answer which tempted one to quarrel outright. I have learned in knocking about the world not to be very squeamish or particular, but really it made my blood run cold to hear the drivers on this mail blaspheme at their horses, each other, their passengers, everything and everybody. I did not think the English language could have furnished such epithets and terms; nor could anything exceed the barbarity with which they treated their horses, which were after the first stage wretched animals, in no sort of condition, and as wretchedly equipped. It was impossible to look without shuddering at the state of their shoulders and withers, which were generally little better than one great festering wound, and nothing but the most unsparing application of the whip would have got them into motion at all.

The vehicle was of course a very light one for four horses if the roads had been of the ordinary kind; as it was, however, there was always as much as they could do, and generally rather more. Each driver worked the mail for about ten hours, and then, with hardly any rest, drove the return mail back again. In returning, I sat beside one who, by the time we got to Penrith, had driven without intermission for 27 hours. When I say 'without intermission', I should add that he had stopped for periods varying from five minutes to half an hour at every single public-house he passed in those 27 hours, *i.e.* probably about 40, the result of which naturally was, that during the latter part of his drive he was more than half drunk and fast asleep.

On the whole, I may say I have seen the public carriages of a good many countries, some of them not very far advanced in civilization; but in discomfort, insecurity, unpunctuality, and general barbarism, the mail between Bathurst and Sydney far surpasses them all. It professed in Sydney to arrive at Bathurst at 6 p.m., *i.e.* 25 hours and a half from Sydney. But we 'knocked up' on the road (every second day, at least, they either 'knock up' or 'break down') and the passengers had to walk four miles to the next stage, from whence we sent back fresh horses to the mail. The result of this, and of some minor accidents, was, that we were four hours late, and did not get to Bathurst till ten.

EMILY SOLDENE
A Dare-devil Driver

Emily Soldene (1844–1912) is little known today; but her fine mezzo-soprano voice and a vivacious acting style won acclaim in the London music-halls of her time and paved the way for a successful career in light opera. She toured in America and Australia; and subsequently settled in Sydney for a time, where she worked as a journalist. She published a book of reminiscences, Theatrical and Musical Recollections, *from which the following description of a coach-ride from Sydney to Melbourne is taken.*

Most of the company went to Melbourne by steamer, and got stuck in the mud outside that charming city, but four of us went overland. Such a journey, on a 'Cobbs' coach, drawn by six young horses, who galloped up mountains and flew down them, driven by coachmen more or less under the influence of the weather! One told us he had been out on a 'burst to a wedding, not slept for three nights', but should be all right when he had had a 'nobbler'. We looked forward with much pleasurable anticipation to the 'nobbler', but were horrified when we saw it—'half a tumbler of whisky'. Our driver tossed it off. He had not overstated its merits. It pulled him together splendidly, not that it made any difference in his driving, which was dare-devil and perfect, as was that of all the other boys. Fancy a track of soft sand, cut into deep ruts, piled high up in the banks, winding in and out huge trees, sharp corners, unexpected fallen trunks, monster up-turned roots, every kind of obstacle, six horses always galloping, the coach banging, creaking, swaying from side to side! Then suddenly down we go, down over a mountain as steep as the side of a house, down into and through a rushing, roaring,

tumbling, bumping, yellow river! Splash, dash. Then with a
'Houp!' 'Hi!' and a big lurch, out again and up the opposite side,
galloping always galloping, breathless; the driver shouting,
cracking his whip, and the horses shaking the water from their
sides, tossing their heads, and jingling their harness; then out on
to the level, soft and springy, covered with mossy turf and
beautiful trees like an English park; away over more sand, and
leaving the mossy turf, and plunging through sharp, cutting, stiff,
rusty-looking, tall grass, growing in huge tufts, far apart. At last
we come to a hut, full gallop, and the driver, without any
preparation, pulls the cattle up on their haunches, and you might
cover them with a blanket, as the saying is. It was all lovely
except for the jolting, and my hands were blistered with holding
on. I liked to sit on the box, though it made one sick, not with
fright exactly, but with excitement and the anticipation of some
possible calamity.

My first flock of flying cockatoos disappointed me dreadfully.
They looked exactly like a flock of pigeons. The driver told me
that when one was wounded or hurt, and could not go on, the
others despatched him, pecked his eyes out and tore him to
pieces. I fancy I have seen something like that in more civilized
regions. We went through groves, forests of gum trees, where
there was no shade, but a delicious perfume. At night we heard
the laughing jackasses, making an awful noise, but they laughed
so well, that we joined in. That's another circumstance I've
noticed in more civilized regions. At Gundagai there is an
immensely long bridge, and we galloped over it in style. The
approach to Gundagai, like every other mining town I have ever
seen, was distinguished by a marvellous display of rubbish of all
sorts, old boots, tin cans of every description (they do say the
goats live on tin cans), meat cans, fish cans, fruit cans, old stays,
old bonnets, old hats, old stockings, heaps of more cans, strewn
for miles. It takes all the romance out of the scene. Gundagai was
surrounded by large, middling, and small heaps of pale red sand;
the place was full of 'holes in the ground', empty holes in the
ground, as if herds of gigantic fox-terriers had been hunting out

their best rabbits. This is the sign of deserted gold-diggings. Can anything be more lonely or more miserable? Nothing. I have seen them in gullies in America, in gullies and plains in Australia, in the heart of the mountains of California, in secret places of the Sierras, in little desert places in Nevada. But they are all alike – miserable, lonely, deserted, except by the wily, patient Chinaman, who goes over again the much gone over ground, making a Celestial's fortune out of the white devil's leavings, and disputing with the thin-legged, big-bellied, bearded goats, the abandoned tin cans. Still, at Gundagai there was a nice hotel. We had boiled fowls for dinner, and I left behind something I prized very much, a 5-cent palm leaf fan I had carried all the way from Cincinnati.

'ROLF BOLDREWOOD' (THOMAS A. BROWNE)
Dick Marston's First Coach Robbery

From Robbery Under Arms: A Story of Life and Adventure in the Bush and in the Goldfields of Australia *(London, 1888). This novel, the most notable of the fictional works of 'Rolf Boldrewood', presents, with a wealth of authentic background detail, the kind of life led by cattle-thieves (duffers) and bushrangers in the 1860s. The action is seen through the eyes of Dick Marston, who, like his father, is a member of a gang of outlaws led by Captain Starlight. Two episodes have been selected from this novel. The first sees the young Marston as a novice coach-robber; the second depicts a more experienced Marston engaged with the gang in the hold-up of a gold-escort coach at Eugowra Rocks. This latter episode is based on the true-life robbing of a gold-escort at Eugowra Rocks by the Gardiner-Ben Hall gang in June, 1862.*

The action in these excerpts takes place in New South Wales.

———————

Our first try-on in the coach line was with the Goulburn mail. We knew the road pretty well, and picked out a place where they had to go slow and couldn't get off the road on either side. There's always places like that in a coach road near the coast, if you look sharp and lay it out beforehand. This wasn't on the track to the diggings, but we meant to leave that alone till we got our hand in a bit. There was a lot of money flying about the country in a general way where there was no sign of gold. All the storekeepers began to get up fresh goods, and to send money in notes and cheques to pay for them. The price of stock kept dealers and fat cattle buyers moving, who had their pockets full of notes as often as not.

Just as you got nearly through Bargo Bush on the old road there was a stiffish hill that the coach passengers mostly walked up, to save the horses—fenced in, too, with a nearly new three-rail fence, all ironbark, and not the sort of thing that you could ride or drive over handy. We thought this would be as good a place as we could pick, so we laid out the whole thing as careful as we could beforehand.

The three of us started out from the Hollow as soon as we could see in the morning; a Friday it was, I remember it pretty well—good reason I had, too. Father and Warrigal went up the night before with the horses we were to ride. They camped about 20 miles on the line we were going, at a place where there was good feed and water, but well out of the way and on a lonely road. There had been an old sheep station there and a hut, but the old man had been murdered by the hut-keeper for some money he had saved, and a story got up that it was haunted by his ghost. It was known as the 'Murdering Hut,' and no shepherd would ever live there after, so it was deserted. We weren't afraid of shepherds alive or dead, so it came in handy for us, as there was water and feed in an old lambing paddock. Besides, the road to it was nearly all a lot of rock and scrub from the Hollow, that made it an unlikely place to be tracked from.

Our dodge was to take three quiet horses from the Hollow and ride them there, first thing; then pick up our own three—Rainbow and two other out-and-outers—and ride bang across the southern road. When things were over we were to start straight back to the Hollow. We reckoned to be safe there before the police had time to know which way we'd made.

It all fitted in first-rate. We cracked on from the Hollow in the morning early, and found Dad and Warrigal all ready for us. The horses were in great buckle, and carried us over to Bargo easy enough before dark. We camped about a mile away from the road, in as thick a place as we could find, where we made ourselves as snug as things would allow. We had brought some grub with us and a bottle of grog, half of which we finished before we started out to spend the evening. We hobbled the horses out and let them have an hour's picking. They were likely to want all they could get before they saw the Hollow again.

It was near 12 o'clock when we mounted. Starlight said –

'By Jove, boys, it's a pity we didn't belong to a troop of irregular horse instead of this rotten colonial Dick Turpin business, that one can't help being ashamed of. They would have been delighted to have recruited the three of us, as we ride, and our horses are worth best part of ten thousand rupees. What a tent-pegger Rainbow would have made, eh, old boy?' he said, patting the horse's neck. 'But Fate won't have it, and it's no use whining.'

The coach was to pass half-an-hour after midnight. An awful long time to wait, it seemed. We finished the bottle of brandy, I know. I thought they never would come, when all of a sudden we saw the lamp.

Up the hill they came slow enough. About half-way up they stopped, and most of the passengers got out and walked up after her. As they came closer to us we could hear them laughing and talking and skylarking, like a lot of boys. They didn't think who was listening. 'You won't be so jolly in a minute or two,' I thinks to myself.

They were near the top when Starlight sings out, 'Stand! Bail up!' and the three of us, all masked, showed ourselves. You never saw a man look so scared as the passenger on the box-seat, a stout, jolly commercial, who'd been giving the coachman Havana cigars, and yarning, and nipping with him at every house they passed. Bill Webster, the driver, pulls up all standing when he sees what was in Starlight's hand, and holds the reins so loose for a minute I thought they'd drop out of his hands. I went up to the coach. There was no one inside—only an old woman and a young one. They seemed struck all of a heap, and couldn't hardly speak for fright.

The best of the joke was that the passengers started running up full split to warm themselves, and came bump against the coach before they found out what was up. One of them had just opened out for a bit of blowing. 'Billy, old man,' he says, 'I'll report you to the Company if you crawl along this way,' when he catches sight of me and Starlight, standing still and silent, with our revolvers pointing his way. By George! I could hardly help laughing. His jaw dropped, and he couldn't get a word out. His throat seemed quite dry.

'Now, gentlemen,' says Starlight, quite cool and cheerful-like, 'you understand her Majesty's mail is stuck up, to use a vulgar expression, and there's no use resisting. I must ask you to stand in a row there by the fence, and hand out all the loose cash, watches, or rings you may have about you. Don't move don't, I say, sir, or I must fire.' (This was to a fidgety, nervous man who couldn't keep quiet.) 'Now, Number One, fetch down the mail bags; Number Two, close up here.'

Here Jim walked up, revolver in hand, and Starlight begins at the first man, very stern –

'Hand out your cash; keep back nothing, if you value your life.'

You never saw a man in such a funk. He was a storekeeper, we found afterwards. He nearly dropped on his knees. Then he handed Starlight a bundle of notes, a gold watch, and took a handsome diamond ring from his finger. This Starlight put into his pocket. He handed the notes and watch to Jim, who had a leather bag ready for them. The man sank down to the ground; he had fainted.

He was left to pick himself up. Number two was told to shell out. They all had something. Some had sovereigns, some had notes and small cheques, which are good in a country place. The squatters draw too many to know the numbers of half that are out, so there's no great chance of their being stopped. There were 18 male passengers, besides the chap on the box-seat. We made him come down. By the time we'd got through them all it was best part of an hour.

I pulled the mail bags through the fence and put them under a tree. Then Starlight went to the coach where the two women were. He took of his hat and bowed.

'Unpleasant necessity, madame, most painful to my feelings altogether, I assure you. I must really ask you – ah – is the young lady your daughter, madame?'

'Not at all,' says the oldest, stout, middle-aged woman; 'I

never set eyes on her before.'

'Indeed, madame,' says Starlight, bowing again; 'excuse my curiosity, I am desolated, I assure you, but may I trouble you for your watches and purses?'

'As you're a gentleman,' said the fat lady, 'I fully expected you'd have let us off. I'm Mrs. Buxter, of Bobbrawobbra.'

'Indeed! I have no words to express my regret,' says Starlight; 'but, my dear lady, hard necessity compels me. Thanks, very much,' he said to the young girl.

She handed over a small old Geneva watch and a little purse. The plump lady had a gold watch with a chain and purse to match.

'Is that all?' says he, trying to speak stern.

'It's my very all,' says the girl, 'five pounds. Mother gave me her watch, and I shall have no money to take me to Bowning, where I am going to a situation.'

Her lips shook and trembled and the tears came into her eyes.

Starlight carefully handed Mrs Buxter's watch and purse to Jim. I saw him turn round and open the other purse, and he put something in, if I didn't mistake. Then he looked in again.

'I'm afraid I'm rather impertinent,' says he, 'but your face, Miss–ah–Elmsdale, thanks–reminds me of someone in another world–the one I once lived in. Allow me to enjoy the souvenir and to return your effects. No thanks; that smile is ample payment. Ladies, I wish you a pleasant journey.'

He bowed. Mrs Buxter did not smile, but looked cross enough at the young lady, who, poor thing, seemed pretty full up and inclined to cry at the surprise.

'Now then, all aboard,' sings out Starlight; 'get in, gentlemen, our business matters are concluded for the night. Better luck next time, William, you had better drive on. Send back from the next stage, and you will find the mail bags under that tree. They shall not be injured more than can be helped. Good-night!'

The driver gathered up his reins and shouted to his team, that was pretty fresh after their spell, and went off like a shot. We sat down by the roadside with one of the coach lamps that we had boned and went through all the letters, putting them back after we'd opened them, and popping all notes, cheques, and bills into Jim's leather sack. We did not waste more time over our letter-sorting than we could help, you bet; but we were pretty well paid for it – better than the post-office clerks are, by all accounts. We left all the mail bags in a heap under the tree, as Starlight had told the driver; and then, mounting our horses, rode as hard as we could lick to where Dad and Warrigal were camped.

When we overhauled the leather sack into which Jim had stowed all the notes and cheques we found that we'd done better than we expected, though we could see from the first it wasn't going to be a bad night's work. We had £370 in notes and gold, a biggish bag of silver, a lot of cheques – some of which would be sure to be paid – seven gold watches and a lot of silver ones, some pretty good. Mrs Buxter's watch was a real beauty, with a stunning chain. Starlight said he should like to keep it himself, and then I knew Bella Barnes was in for a present. Starlight was one of those chaps that never forget any kind of promise he'd once made. Once he said a thing it would be done as sure as death—if he was alive to do it; and many a time I've known him to take the greatest lot of trouble, no matter how pushed he might be, to carry out something which another man would have never troubled his head about.

We got safe to the Murdering Hut, and a precious hard ride it was, and tried our horses well, for, mind you, they'd been under saddle best part of 24 hours when we got back, and had done a good deal over a hundred miles. We made a short halt while the tea was boiling, then we all separated for fear a black tracker might have been loosed on our trail, and knowing well what blood-hounds they are sometimes.

Warrigal and Starlight went off together as usual; they were pretty safe to be out of harm's way. Father made off on a line of his own. We took the two horses we'd ridden out of the Hollow, and made for that place the shortest way we knew. We could afford to hit out—horse-flesh was cheap to us—but not to go slow. Time was more than money to us now—it was blood, or next thing to it.

'ROLF BOLDREWOOD' (THOMAS A. BROWNE)
Bad Day at Eugowra Rocks

A month's loafing in the Hollow. Nothing doing and nothing to think of except what was miserable enough, God knows. Then things began to shape themselves, in a manner of speaking. We didn't talk much together; but each man could see plain enough what the others were thinking of. Dad growled out a word now and then, and Warrigal would look at us from time to time with a flash in his hawk's eyes that we'd seen once or twice before and knew the meaning of. As for Jim, we were bound to do something or other, if it was only to keep him from going melancholy mad. I never seen any man changed more from what he used to be than Jim did. He that was the most careless, happy-go-lucky chap that ever stepped, always in a good temper and full of his larks. At the end of the hottest day in summer on the plains, with no water handy, or the middle of the coldest winter night in an ironbark forest, and we sitting on our horses waiting for daylight, with the rain pouring down our backs, not game to light a fire, and our hands that cold we could hardly hold the reins, it was all one to Jim. Always jolly, always ready to make little of it all. Always ready to laugh or chaff or go on with monkey tricks like a boy. Now it was all the other way with him. He'd sit grizzling and smoking by himself all day long. No getting a word out of him. The only time he seemed to brighten up was once when he got a letter from Jeanie. He took it away into the bush and stayed hours and hours.

From never thinking about anything or caring what came upper-most, he seemed to have changed all on the other tack and do nothing but think. I'd seen a chap in Berrima something like him for a month or two; one day he manned the barber's razor and cut his throat. I began to be afraid Jim would go off his head and blow his brains out with his own revolver. Starlight himself got to be cranky and restless-like, too. One night he broke out as we were standing smoking under a tree, a mile or so from the cave:

'By all the devils, Dick, I can't stand this sort of thing much longer. We shall go mad or drink ourselves to death' – (we'd all been pretty well 'on' the night before) – 'if we stick here till we're trapped or smoked out like a 'guana out of a tree spout. We must make a rise somehow, and try for blue water again. I've been fighting against the notion the whole time we've been here, but the devil and your old dad (who's a near relative, I believe) have been too strong for us. Of course you know what it's bound to be?'

'I suppose so. I know when dad was away last week he saw that beggar and some of his mates. They'd partly made it up a while back, but didn't fancy doing it altogether by themselves. They've been waiting on the chance of our standing in and your taking command.'

'Of course, the old story,' he says, throwing his cigar away, and giving a half laugh—such a laugh it was, too. 'Captain Starlight again, I suppose. The paltry vanity of leadership, and of being in the front of my fellow-men, has been the ruin of me ever since I could recollect. If my people had let me go into the army, as I begged and prayed of them to do, it might have been all the other way. I recollect that day and hour when my old governor refused my boyish petition, laughed at me—sneered at me. I took the wrong road then. I swear to you, Dick, I never had thought of evil till that cursed day which made me reckless and indifferent to everything. And this is the end—a wasted life, a felon's doom! Quite melodramatic, isn't it, Richard? Well, we'll play out the last act with spirit. "Enter first robber," and so on. Good-night.'

He walked away. I never heard him say so much about himself before. It set me thinking of what luck and chance there seemed to be in this world. How men were not let do what they knew was best for 'em—often and often—but something seemed to drive 'em farther and farther along the wrong road, like a lot of stray wild cattle that wants to make back to their own run, and a dog here, a fence the other way, a man on foot or a flock of sheep always frightening 'em farther and farther from the old beat till they get back into a bit of back country or mallee scrub and stop there for good. Cattle and horses and men and women are awful like one another in their ways, and the more you watch 'em the more it strikes you.

Another day or two idling and card-playing, another headache after too much grog at night, brought up to a regular go in about business, and then we fixed it for good.

We were to stick up the next monthly gold escort. That was all. We knew it would be a heavy one and trusted to our luck to get clear off with the gold, and then take a ship for Honolulu or San Francisco. A desperate chance; but we were desperate men. We had tried to work hard and honest. We had done so for best part of a year. No one could say we had taken the value of a half-penny from any man. And yet we were not let stay right when we asked for nothing but to be let alone and live out the rest of our lives like men.

They wouldn't have us that way, and now they must take us across the grain, and see what they would gain by that. So it happened we went out one day with Warrigal to show us the way, and after riding for hours and hours, we came to a thick scrub. We rode through it till we came to an old cattle track. We followed that till we came to a tumbledown slab hut with a stockyard beside it. The yard had been mended, and the rails were up. Seven or eight horses were inside, all in good condition. As many men were sitting or standing about smoking outside the old hut.

When we rode up they all came forward and we had it out. We knew who was coming and were ready for 'em. There was Moran, of course, quiet and savage-looking, just as like a black snake as ever, twisting about with his deadly glittering eyes, wanting to bite someone. There was Daly and Burke, Wall and Hulbert, and two or three more—I won't say who they were now—and if you please who should come out of the hut last but

Master Billy the Boy, as impudent as you like, with a pipe in his mouth, and a revolver in his belt, trying to copy Moran and Daly. I felt sorry when I see him, and thought what he'd gradually come to bit by bit, and where he'd most likely end, all along of the first money he had from father for telegraphing. But after all I've a notion that men and women grow up as they are intended to from the beginning. All the same as a tree from seed. You may twist it this road or that, make it a bit bigger or smaller according to the soil or the way it's pruned and cut down when it's young, but you won't alter the nature of that tree or the fruit that it bears. You won't turn a five-corner into a quince, or a geebung into an orange, twist and twine, and dig and water as you like. So whichever way Billy the Boy had been broken and named he'd have bolted and run off the course. Take a pet dingo now. He might look very tame and follow them that feed him, and stand the chain; but as soon as anything passed close that he could kill, he'd have his teeth into it and be lapping its blood before you could say 'knife,' and the older he got the worse he'd be.

'Well, Dick,' says this young limb of Satan, 'so you've took to the Queen's highway again, as the chap says in the play. I thought you and Jim was a-going to jine the Methodies or the Sons of Temperance at Turon, you both got to look so thunderin' square on it. Poor old Jim looks dreadful down in the mouth, don't he, though?'

'It would be all the better for you if you'd joined some other body, you young scamp,' I said. 'Who told you to come here? I've half a mind to belt you home again to your mother'; and I walked towards him.

'No, you won't, Dick Marston, don't you make any mistake,' says the young bull-pup, looking nasty. 'I'm as good a man as you, with this little tool.' Here he pulled out his revolver. 'I've as much right to turn out as you have. What odds is it to you what I do?'

I looked rather foolish at this, and Moran and Burke began to laugh.

'You'd better set up a night-school, Dick,' says Burke, 'and get Billy and some of the other flash kiddies to come. They might turn over a new leaf in time.'

'If you'll stand up, or Moran there, that's grinning behind you, I'll make some of ye laugh on the wrong side,' I said.

'Come on,' drawls Moran, taking off his coat, and walking up; 'I'd like to have a smack at you before you go into the Church.'

We should have been at it hammer and tongs—we both hated one another like poison—only the others interfered, and Billy said we ought to be ashamed of ourselves for quarrelling like schoolboys. We were nice sort of chaps to stick up a gold escort. That made a laugh, and we knocked off.

Well, it looked as if no one wanted to speak. Then Hulbert, a very quiet chap, says, 'I believe Ben Marston's the oldest man here; let's hear what he's got to say.'

Father gets up at once, and looks steady at the rest of 'em, takes his pipe out of his mouth, and shakes the baccy out. Then he says:

'All on ye knows without my telling what we've come here about, and what there's hangin' to it. It's good enough if it's done to rights; but make no mistake, boys, it's a battle as must be fought game, and right back to the ropes, or not at all. If there's a bird here that won't stand the steel he'd better be put in a bag and took home again.'

'Never mind about the steel, daddy,' says one of the new men. 'We're all good for a flutter when the wager's good. What'll it be worth a man, and where are we going to divide? We know your mob's got some crib up in the mountains that no one knows about. We don't want the swag took there and planted. It mightn't be found easy.'

'Did ever a one of ye heer tell o' me actin' crooked?' says father. 'Look here, Bill, I'm not as young as I was, but you stand up to me for three rounds and I'll take some of the cheek out of yer.'

Bill laughed.

'No fear, daddy, I'd sooner face Dick or Jim. But I only want what's fair between man and man. It's a big touch, you know, and we can't take it to the bank to divide, like diggers, or summons yer either.'

'What's the good of growlin' and snappin?' says Burke. 'We're all goin' in regular, I suppose, share and share alike?' The men nodded. 'Well, there's only one way to make things shipshape, and that's to have a captain. We'll pick one of ourselves, and whatever he says we'll bind ourselves to do – life or death. Is that it, boys?'

'Yes, yes, that's the only way,' came from all hands.

'Now, the next thing to work is who we're to make captain of. There's one here as we can all depend on, who knows more about road-work than all the rest of us put together. You know who I mean; but I don't want ye to choose him or any man because I tell you. I propose Starlight for captain if he'll take it, and them that don't believe me let 'em find a better man if they can.'

'I vote for Dan Moran,' says another man, a youngish farmer-looking chap. 'He's a bushman, like ourselves, and not a half-bred swell, that's just as likely to clear out when we want him most as do anything else.'

'You go back to the Springs and feed them pigs, Johnny,' says father, walking towards the young chap. 'That's about what *you're* bred for; nobody'll take you for a swell, quarter-bred, or anything else. Howsoever, let's draw lots for it. Every man put his fancy down on a bit of paper, and put 'em into my old hat here.'

This was done after a bit, and the end of it was ten votes for Starlight and two or three for Moran, who looked savage and sulkier than ever.

When this was over Starlight walked over from where he was standing, near me and Jim, and faced the crowd. He drew himself up a bit, and looked round as haughty as he used to do when he walked up the big room at the Prospectors' Arms in Turon—as if all the rest of us was dirt under his feet.

'Well, my lads,' he said, 'you've done me the great honour to elect me to be your captain. I'm willing to act, or I shouldn't be here. If you're fools enough to risk your lives and liberties for a thousand ounces of gold a man, I'm fool enough to show you the way.'

'Hurrah!' said half-a-dozen of them, flinging up their hats. 'We're on, Captain. Starlight for ever! You ride ahead and we'll back up.'

'That will do,' he says, holding up his hand as if to stop a lot of dogs barking; 'but listen to me.' Here he spoke a few words in that other voice of his that always sounded to me and Jim as if it was a different man talking, or the devil in his likeness. 'Now mind this before we go: you don't quite know me; you will by and by, perhaps. When I take command of this gang, for this bit of work or any other, my word's law—do you hear? And if any man disputes it or disobeys my orders, by—, I'll shoot him like a dog.'

As he stood there looking down on the lot of 'em, as if he was their king, with his eyes burning up at last with that slow fire that lay at the bottom of 'em. and only showed out sometimes, I couldn't help thinking of a pirate crew that I'd read of when I was a boy, and the way the pirate captain ruled 'em.

We were desperately fidgety and anxious till the day came. Whilst we were getting ready two or three things went wrong, of course. Jim got a letter from Jeanie, all the way from Melbourne, where she'd gone. It seems she'd got her money from the bank— Jim's share of the gold—all right. She was a saving, careful little woman, and she told him she'd enough to keep them both well for four or five years, anyhow. What she wanted him to do was to promise that he'd never be mixed up in any more dishonest work, and to come away down to her at once.

'It was the easiest thing in the world, she said, 'to get away from Melbourne to England or America. Ships were going every day, and glad to take any man that was strong and willing to work his passage for nothing; they'd pay him besides.'

She'd met one or two friends down there as would do anything to help her and him. If he would only get down to Melbourne all would yet be well; but she begged and prayed him, if he loved her, and for the sake of the life she hoped to live with him yet, to come away from his companions and take his own Jeanie's advice, and try and do nothing wrong for the future.

If Jim had got his letter before we made up matters, just at the

last he'd have chucked up the sponge and cleared out for good
and all. He as good as said so; but he was one of them kind of men
that once he'd made a start never turned back. There'd been
some chaff, to make things worse, between Moran and Daly, and
some of the other fellows about being game and what not,
specially after what father said at the hut, so he wouldn't draw
out of it now.

I could see it fretted him worse than anything since we came
back, but he filled himself up with the idea that we'd be sure to
get the gold all right, and clear out different ways to the coast,
and then we'd have something worth while leaving off with.
Another thing, we'd been all used to having what money we
wanted lately, and we none of us fancied living like poor men
again in America or anywhere else. We hadn't had hardly a scrap
from Aileen since we'd come back this last time. It wasn't much
odds. She was regular broken-hearted; you could see it in every
line.

'She had been foolish enough to hope for better things,' she
said; 'now she expected nothing more in this world, and was
contented to wear out her miserable life the best way she could. If
it wasn't that her religion told her it was wrong, and that mother
depended on her, she'd drown herself in the creek before the
door. She couldn't think why some people were brought into this
miserable world at all. Our family had been marked out to evil,
and the same fate would follow us to the end. She was sorry for
Jim, and believed if he had been let take his own road that he
would have been happy and prosperous to-day. It was a pity he
could not have got away safely to Melbourne with his wife before
that wicked woman, who deserved to be burnt alive, ruined
everything. Even now we might all escape, the country seemed in
so much confusion with all the strangers and bad people' (bad
people—well, everyone thinks their own crow the blackest) 'that
the goldfields had brought into it, that it wouldn't be hard to get
away in a ship somehow. If nothing else bad turned up perhaps it
might come to pass yet.'

This was the only writing we'd had from poor Aileen. It began all misery and bitterness, but got a little better at the end. If she and Gracey could have got hold of Kate Morrison there wouldn't have been much left of her in a quarter of an hour, I could see that.

Inside was a little bit of paper with one line, 'For my sake,' that was all. I knew the writing; there was no more. I could see what Gracey meant, and wished over and over again that I had the chance of going straight, as I'd wished a thousand times before, but it was too late, too late! When the coach is running down hill and the brake's off, it's no use trying to turn. We had all our plan laid out and settled to the smallest thing. We were to meet near Eugowra Rocks a good hour or two before the escort passed, so as to have everything ready. I remember the day as well as if it was yesterday. We were all in great buckle and very fit, certainly. I don't think I ever felt better in my life. There must be something out-and-out spiriting in a real battle when a bit of a scrimmage like this sent our blood boiling through our veins; made us feel as if we weren't plain Dick and Jim Marston, but regular grand fellows, in a manner of speaking. What fools men are when they're young–and sometimes after that itself–to be sure.

We started at daylight, and only stopped once on the road for a bite for ourselves and to water the horses, so that we were in good time. We brought a little corn with us, just to give the horses something; they'd be tied up for hours and hours when we got to the place pitched on. They were all there before us; they hadn't as good horses by a long chalk as we had, and two of their packers were poor enough. Jim and I were riding ahead with Starlight a little on the right of us. When the fellows saw Rainbow they all came crowding round him as if he'd been a show.

'By George!' says Burke, 'that's a horse worth calling a horse, Captain. I often heard tell of him, but never set eyes on him before. I've two minds to shake him and leave you my horse and a share of the gold to boot. I never saw his equal in my life, and I've seen some plums, too.

'Honour among–well–bush-rangers, eh, Burke?' says Starlight cheerily. 'He's the right sort, isn't he? We shall want good goers to-night. Are we all here now? We'd better get to business.'

Yes, they were all there, a lot of well-built, upstanding chaps, young and strong, and fit to do anything that a man could do in the way of work or play. It was a shame to see them there (and us, too, for the matter of that), but there was no get away now. There will be fools and rogues to the end of the world, I expect. Even Moran looked a bit brighter than he did last time. He was one of those chaps that a bit of real danger smartens up. As for Burke, Daly, and Hulbert, they were like a lot of schoolboys, so full of their fun and larks.

Starlight just spoke a word to them all; he didn't talk much, but looked hard and stern about the face, as a captain ought to do. He rode up to the gap and saw where the trees had been cut down to block up the road. It would be hard work getting the coach through there now–for a bit to come.

After that our horses and the two packers were left behind with Warrigal and father, close enough for hearing, but well out of the way for seeing; it was behind a thick belt of timber. They tied up some to trees and short-hobbled others, keeping them all so as to be ready at a moment's notice. Our men hid themselves behind rocks and stumps on the high side of the road so as they could see well, and had all the shadow on their side. Wall and Hulbert and their lot had their mob of horses, packers, and all planted away, and two young fellows belonging to their crowd minding them.

We'd been ready a good bit when a cove comes tearing up full bat. We were watching to see how he shaped, and whether he looked likely to lay on the police, when I saw it was Billy the Boy.

'Now I call this something like,' says he, pulling up short; 'army in readiness, the enemy not far off. My word, it is a fine thing to turn out, ain't it, Dick? Do you chaps feel shaky at all? Ain't yer gallied the least little bit? They're a-comin'!'

'How long will they be?' Starlight said. 'Just remember that you're not skylarking at a pound-yard, my boy.'

'All right, Captain,' he answered, quiet enough. 'I started on ahead the moment I saw 'em leave the camp. They're safe to be here in ten minutes now. You can see 'em when they came into the flat. I'll clear out to the back for a bit. I want 'em to think I come up permiskus-like when it's over.' So the young rascal galloped away till the trees hid him, and in a quarter of an hour more we saw the leaders of the four-horse drag that carried the escort gold turn round on the forest road and show out into the flat.

It gave me a queer feeling just at first. We hadn't been used to firing on the Queen's servants, not in cold blood, anyhow, but it was them or us for it now. There was no time to think about it. They came along at a steady trot up the hill. We knew the Turon sergeant of police that drove, a tall man with a big black beard down to his chest. He had been in an English dragoon regiment, and could handle the ribbons above a bit. He had a trooper alongside him on the box with his rifle between his knees. Two more were in the body of the drag. They had put their rifles down and were talking and laughing, not expecting anything sudden. Two more of the mounted men rode in front, but not far. The couple behind were a good way off. All of a sudden the men in front came on the trees lying across the road. They pulled up short, and one of them jumped down and looked to see if anything could be done to move them. The other man held his horse. The coach drove up close, so that they were bunched up pretty well together.

'Who the devil has been doing that?' sung out the sergeant. 'Just as if the road isn't bad enough without these infernal lazy scoundrels of bullock-drivers cutting down trees to make us go round. It's a beastly track here at the best of times.'

'I believe them trees have been fallen on purpose,' says the trooper that was down. 'There's been men, and horses, too, about here to-day, by the tracks. They're up to no good!'

'Fire!'

The order was given in Starlight's clear, bold voice. Just like a horn it sounded. You might have heard it twice as far off. A dozen shots followed the next second, making as much row as fifty because of the way the sound echoed among the rocks.

I never saw a bigger surprise in my life, and wasn't likely to do, as this was my first regular battle. We had plenty of time to take aim, and just at first it looked as if the whole blessed lot of the police was killed and wounded.

The sergeant threw up his arms and fell off the box like a log, just under the horses' feet. One of the troopers on ahead dropped, he that was holding the horses, and both horses started off at full gallop. The two men in the body of the drag were both hit—one badly. So when the two troopers came at full gallop from the back they found us cutting the traces of the team, that was all plunging like mad, and letting the horse go.

We opened fire at them directly they showed themselves; of course they couldn't do much in the face of a dozen men, all well armed and behind good cover. They kept it up for a bit till one of their horses was hit, and then made tracks for Turon to report that the escort had been stuck up by 20 or 30 men at Eugowra Rocks—the others had come up with the pack-horses by this time, along with Master Billy the Boy firing his revolver and shouting enough for half-a-dozen; so we looked a big crowd—that all the men were shot dead, wounded, or taken prisoners, and that a strong force had better be despatched at once to recapture the gold.

A good deal of this was true, though not all. The only man killed was the sergeant. He was shot clean through the heart, and never stirred again. Of the five other men, three was badly wounded and two slightly. We attended to them as well as we could, and tied the others so that they would not be able to give any bother for an hour or two at any rate.

Then the trouble began about dividing the gold. We opened the sort of locker that there was in the centre of the coach and took out the square boxes of gold. They held canvas bags, all labelled and weighed to the grain, of about 1,000 oz. each. There were 14 boxes in all. Not a bad haul.

Some of the others couldn't read or write, and they wouldn't trust us, so they brought their friend with them, who was an educated man sure enough. We were a bit stunned to see him, holding the sort of position he did at the Turon. But there he was, and he did his work well enough. He brought a pair of scales with him and weighed the lot, and portioned it all out amongst us just the same as Mr Scott, the banker, used to do for us at the Turon when we brought in our month's washing-up. We had 5,000 oz. Starlight had an extra share on account of being captain, and the rest had somewhere about 8,000 oz. or 9,000 oz. among them. It wasn't so bad.

Dad wasn't long before he had our lot safely packed and on his two pack-horses. Warrigal and he cleared out at a trot, and went out of sight in a jiffy. It was every man for himself now. We waited a bit to help them with their swag; it was awful heavy. We told them that their pack-horses would never carry it if there was anything of a close run for it.

'Suppose you think you've got the only good horse in the country, Dick Marston,' says Daly. 'We'll find a horse to run anything you've got, barrin' Rainbow. I've got a little roan horse here as shall run ever a horse ye own, for three mile, for a hundred notes, with 12 stone up. What do you think of that, now?'

'Don't take your shirt off, Patsey,' I said. 'I know the roan's as good as ever was foaled' (so he was; the police got him after Patsey was done for, and kept him till he died of old age), 'but he's in no condition. I'm talking of the pack-horses; they're not up to much, as you'll find out.'

We didn't want to rush off at once, for fear the other fellows might say something afterwards if anything happened cross. So we saw them make a fair start for a spot on Weddin Mountain, where they thought they were right. We didn't think we could be caught once we made tracks in earnest. After a couple or three hours' riding we should be pretty safe, and daylight would see us at the Hollow.

We stopped, besides, to do what we could for the wounded men. There were none of them regularly done for, except the sergeant. One man was shot through the lungs, and was breathing out blood every now and then. We gave them some brandy and water, and covered them all up and left them as comfortable as we could. Besides that, we sent Billy the Boy, who couldn't be recognised, to the camp to have a doctor sent as soon as possible. Then we cleared and started off, not the way we had to go, but so as we could turn into it.

We couldn't ride very slow after such a turn as that, so we made the pace pretty hot for the first 20 miles or so. By Jove! it was a great ride; the forest was middling open, and we went three parts speed when we could see before us. The horses seemed to go as if they knew there was something up. I can see Rainbow now, swinging along with that beautiful bounding style of going he had, snorting now and then and sending out his legs as if one hundred miles, more or less, was nothing. His head up, his eye shining like a star, his nostrils open, and every now and then, if anything got up, he'd give a snort as if he'd just come up out of the bush. They'd had a longish day and a fast ride before they got to Eugowra, just enough to eat to keep them from starving, with a drink of water. Now they were going the same style back, and they'd never had the saddles off their backs. All the night through we rode before we got to the top of Nulla Mountain; very glad to see it we were then. We took it easy for a few miles now and again, then we'd push on again. We felt awful sleepy at times; we'd been up and at it since the morning before; long before daylight, too. The strangeness and the chance of being followed kept us up, else I believe we'd have dropped off our horses' backs, regular dead beat.

We lost ground now and then through Warrigal not being there to guide us, but Jim took the lead and he wasn't far out; besides, the horses knew which way to steer for their grasses at the Hollow. They wouldn't let us go much off the line if it was ever so dark. We gave 'em their heads mostly. The sun was just rising as we rode across the last tableland. We got off and stumbled along, horses and men, down the track to the Hollow. Dad and Warrigal hadn't come back; of course they couldn't stand the pace we did. They'd have to camp for a bit, but they both knew of plants and hiding holes, where all the police in the colony couldn't find them. We knew they'd turn up some time next day. So we let go our horses, and after bit of supper laid down and slept till well on the afternoon.

When I looked round I saw the dog sleeping at Jim's feet, old Crib. He never left father very far, so of course the old man must be home, or pretty close up. I was that dead beat and tired out that I turned over and went to sleep for another couple of hours, when I next woke up I was right and felt rested, so I put on my things, had a good wash, and went out to speak to father. He was sitting by the fire outside smoking, just as if he'd never been away.

BILL WANNAN

A Coach Crash ends James
Bonwick's Career

While James Bonwick, author of many books of Australiana and an Inspector of Schools in Western Victoria, was on a tour of duty during 1869, he found it necessary to take a Cobb & Co. coach to one particular school which was in a remote corner of the Ballarat district.

Despite the skill and venturesomeness of the coach driver there was an accident. Bonwick later wrote: 'Attempting to drive over a wet log, we skidded and the huge vehicle came down with a crash. Very much shaken the roll-over affected my head to the finishing stroke. But by strong efforts of will I succeeded in reaching the manse of that brilliant Presbyterian minister the Rev William Henderson of Ballaarat where I collapsed.'

Bonwick suffered severe injuries which effectively put an end to his career as a schools inspector. It had been necessary for him to reach most parts of his area on horseback. But the accident caused him to give up horse riding for ever, 'from my liability to fall in a sudden head attack.'

WILLIAM DERRINCOURT (alias W. DAY)
Confessions of a Bushranger

The following true narrative gives a graphic picture of what highway robbery, in nineteenth-century New South Wales, was really like, as seen through the eyes of a robber. It is from Old Convict Days, *edited by Louis Becke (London, 1899). I have used here the excerpt given by Nancy Keesing in her fine anthology,* Gold Fever *(Sydney, 1967). The Miller-Macartney bibliography,* Australian Literature *(1956), gives the name of the 'presumed' author of* Old Convict Days *as 'William Derricourt' or 'Day', and notes: 'edited with introduction, some annotations, and a conclusion by Becke.' For some fascinating biographical material about 'Derrincourt' or 'Derricourt' the reader is referred to* Gold Fever.

────────────

I now received a letter from my former manager on the Turon (R. Wilson), informing me that he had lost all his savings in a fishery speculation, and asking me to provide him with funds for his return to the goldfields. I sent him £20, on the understanding that when he arrived he was to work for me at £3 per week, and repay me £1 per week. . . . I had built another house on the opposite side of the road from my first one . . . and this I arranged to let Wilson have on his arrival, which shortly took place.

To my surprise I found he had brought a young wife with him, so I furnished his new abode and made it comfortable for him. Wilson had not been long located with me when it turned out that his young wife was in the habit of visiting M. Kilreavy's public-house, close at hand, for drink, and bringing it home. After a time I found my wife had been induced to join her in her cups; indeed, on one occasion I found the two on the floor dancing 'Jack's the Lad' to their own music, and no dinner cooked.

Before the advent of Wilson's wife my old woman was noted as a hard-working woman, attentive to her household duties, and a kind and affectionate mother; but now these orgies were of daily occurrence, and how to mend matters puzzled me. At length I proposed to give Wilson the same wages, and forgive him the balance of his debt, provided he removed his wife to a safe distance. He was agreeable, but the wife would not stir. . . . At last I called on Mr Johnstone, and stated all the circumstances of my unhappy condition, adding that there was another woman cohabiting with a man some distance off who was as bad as Wilson's wife, and I wanted to try and shift them. Mr Johnstone told me there must be some distinct charge laid against them, otherwise he could not interfere.

I got maddened to such a pitch at their increasing drunken fits that I was almost tempted to bundle them down a hole. One day I went down to the Court, leaving Wilson at work, and on his inquiring on my return where I had been all day, I told him I had been to the Court as bondsman for Kilreavy and O'Brien, the publicans. He asked me when the publicans had to forward the £30 for their licenses to Sydney. I told him by the 1st of July. 'My word, Bill,' he said, 'what a swag of money there must be in the mail about the end of June. I see how we are hampered with these drunken women. I want to get away, but I have not the means of shifting. I'll make a proposal to you. I have been considering. You know I'm an "old hand", and understand the tactics of the game I intend, and you don't.

'Now if you'll find me in arms and rations, and go with me, I'll stick up the mail between Bathurst and Orange. I only want you to be with me to carry off the plunder, which we will share. I'll make off to England after the affair, and you, not being openly in it, can come back here.'

I thought over the matter and replied, 'You see, you have nothing to lose if you are caught, and I have everything.'

'But look at the state you are in now,' he urged. 'You cannot be much worse off than you are now, with these drunken women about you.'

His arguments overcame my scruples, and I consented to join him. We calculated to make our arrangements so as to bring us to the scene of action about the 25th of June. I told him, however, that as we were going in this line [bushranging] we might as well be hung for a sheep as a lamb, and that we ought to go further down on the Sydney Road, so as to intercept the Mudgee as well as the Bathurst mail on the Sydney side of Mount Victoria, past Hartley. . . . We were not to let the women have the least inkling of our designs; but inform them that we were going down to Sydney on business, and would be as expeditious as possible. We concealed away from the house the arms, consisting of a double-barrelled gun, a horse pistol, and a dagger pistol, with some rations, and had about £1 in silver, with a change of clothes. All being prepared, we started on foot early in the morning . . . and wherever we stopped we told the same tale— that we were on our way to Sydney. . . .

[After a tramp of several days] on the Lithgow side of the Sydney Road we found a cave about 100 yards from the road.

At daylight we made everything ready, and took a survey of our surroundings. Standing on Mount Victoria we could see across the Grose Valley . . . a distance of about seven miles in a straight line. On a bare hill we noticed a tree of peculiar shape, which we fixed on as a landmark. We followed on, on this line till we reached the hill and tree, and took a backward survey of the line. Being pretty well sure of the proper direction, we returned in our tracks, breaking down small branches for future guidance.

On our way we had come to a very steep and almost inaccessible gully, deep and narrow. This we spanned by placing one end of a large stout sapling in the fork of a tree, resting the other end in the face of the precipice opposite, in such a manner that in case of being hard pressed we could withdraw this temporary bridge, and so impede the further progress of our pursuers. Near the top of the precipice, which it was impossible to ascend in a straight line, we found a hole through which we could just crawl by putting aside some stones. These stones we could use to block the passage up again with. We now made for our cave near the road, and lit a charcoal fire, made some tea, and had something to eat after our exertions. We then went close to the road and lay in quiet behind some bushes, within earshot of anyone passing. While there two troopers passed from Blackheath to Hartley, chatting away in right merry mood, so, without gaining any information, we went back to the cave to wait for the coming of the coach, about 7 a.m., its usual time of passing the spot.

Dressed in as good guise as possible, with a red comforter pulled over his face, having eye-holes cut out, Wilson got the double gun, and with pistol in belt was prepared for action. While lying in wait we could see the coach, heavily laden with passengers, slowly winding up the foot of the hill about a mile distant. On reaching the steeper part the passengers were seen to dismount, and came straggling up in the wake of the coach. My instructions were to stand aloof, and only appear in case of Wilson seeming to be overpowered. As the coach came up I waited, nervously expecting each moment to hear it stop. But no. It went smoothly and leisurely by, followed by its former occupants. Presently Wilson appeared, shivering from the cold, for the top of Mount Victoria in June is not a very pleasant place in which to remain inactive; but, in my opinion, a modicum of fear had some part in his tremblings. He said it was of no use trying it on this time, as he would have no chance with such a mob of stragglers behind the coach; it was not as if he had them all collected together. A little damped in our expectations, but not defeated, we retired to await the next opportunity; but at the critical moment something of the same sort occurred. We were again baulked, and I began to rail at him for his apparent want of pluck . . . 'the truth is, you haven't the spirit of a cur, you're only a skulk.'

. . . . ' Here we are,' I said, 'with only rations enough for a day, and dare not show ourselves to procure more. Now, tomorrow morning, on the arrival of the mail, I'll go and stop it, if

there are fifty passengers. You go about a half-mile on the road
we have marked out for our escape, and wait there, for you will be
no good to me should they prove too much for me, and if I did
right I would put a ball through you, and leave you to rot
here.'

At six o'clock next morning, when we had eaten the last of our
food, I began to disguise myself. Taking the empty flour bag I
shook it out and drew it over me, so as to have my head in one
corner, where I cut two eye-holes, with two arm-holes in the
sides. I drew the charges of both barrels of the gun, saw that my
powder was perfectly dry, and reloaded. The same with the
pistols. I put slugs in one gun barrel and three pistol balls in the
other, put a strap round the flour bag on my body, and stuck in
the pistols one on each side. The gun I held in my hand. On
looking through the eye-holes I could see Wilson's teeth chatter-
ing in his head, and his whole frame in a shake. My anger was
roused, and between rage and contempt I said, 'Before going out
I have a mind to knock your brains out with the butt of my gun.
What good are you to me? If I had been inclined for this sort of
work, could I not have done it on my own account? But you have
led me into it, and now leave me in the lurch.'

So saying, I started for the road, and he went on the track of
our intended retreat. Crossing the road I got into a drain in the
shape of a horseshoe, about six feet deep in the centre. I had been
thus ensconced about a quarter of an hour when I heard a
creaking, shuffling noise in the road below me; and, peeping over
the bank in front, I saw about sixteen of the road party from
Hartley preparing with their overseer to commence work at this
identical spot. Here was a dilemma. Could I have got cut without
being seen, I would have gone further, either up or down the
road; but this could not be.

While considering my hazardous situation, I heard the sound
of approaching wheels, and knew there was no time to be lost. I
must be prompt and cool; after all my bragging it would not do
now to show the white feather. At the moment the leaders of the
team came opposite my lurking-place I sprang on the bank, and

in a voice of thunder shouted, 'Stop! Anyone that stirs I'll put a ball through.'

The roadmen, hearing this peremptory order, were stupefied, and dropping their tools, stood open-mouthed, and seemingly petrified. The coachman instantly pulled up, and the passengers on foot, straggling up round the elbow of the hill, collected in a group close by. Casting my eye for a moment to my left, but with gun still presented, I spied within twenty feet of me in the drain one of the road party, who had entered it for some purpose of his own, and who, as will be afterwards seen, paid dearly for having so done, but who now, like the rest, seemed paralysed.

Among the passengers was a man of commanding stature and gentlemanly appearance. On the coachman calling to him, 'Look here, sir!' he turned back and went to the leaders' heads.

I sang out to the driver, 'Chuck out these mail bags, and look sharp about it, or I will very quick fetch you off your perch.' He threw out ten bags. Meantime, a batch of newly-arrived Chinamen from Sydney, on their way to the diggings, came up. I ordered them to stand back and not to move. They crowded together in a mob, right in front of the horses, and the way was effectually blocked with their bamboos, baskets, and broad-brimmed hats. They looked like a flock of bewildered sheep.

I then ordered the driver to sound the bottom of the boot with the butt of the whip, and in so doing he touched something, producing no sound. I instantly ordered him, on peril of his life, to throw them out. It proved to be the Mudgee mail bag, most precious of all. Addressing the tall gentleman, I said, 'How now, my long slab, you bundle into the coach and keep yourself quiet, and look sharp or I'll hasten your movements.' He did as told, muttering. The other passengers stood a little distance off, mute as mice, not daring to move, no doubt fearing for their money and valuables, with which I had no intention of interfering. Among them was my old bullock-driver from the Turon, Jem Goodwin, on his way to get married in Sydney. My tall friend being seated, I told the driver to move on and pick up his passengers, and turning to the roadmen ordered them back ten

paces from the bags lying on the ground, and surrounded by the
Chinamen, who had to make way for the coach.

Shouldering the eleven bags, nearly as much as I could carry, I
made for our marked tree line. I afterwards learned that at the
toll-bar the tall man stuck up a bill or placard, offering a reward
of £100 on behalf of the Government for the capture of the
robber. This he had power to do, being no less than Holyoake
Bailey, Esq., the Attorney-General, on his return from the
Mudgee election. The roadmen I had ordered back, fearing a
rush as I picked up the bags. As for the Chinamen, I passed
through among them as a shepherd through his flock, pushing
them aside to make a passage for the bulky load of bags on my
shoulders, and made along the line we had marked out.

On coming to the deep gully that I had bridged over, I
dropped the mail bags down, straddled across my sapling bridge,
and gaining the opposite bank, drew it after me, and launched
into the depths.

I then picked up my bags again and made for the hole in the
ascent, which, had I missed, I could not have got up the steep
bank. At the top at last, I retreated two or three hundred yards
into a thick scrub, cut the bags open, and bundled the contents
out in a heap. I selected all the letters and everything I thought of
value, depositing them in one bag, and leaving behind all
newspapers and bulky articles seemingly worthless. My load was
now necessarily greatly lightened, and even up to now I wonder
how I managed to get along so well under such a weight of leather
and paper. . . . I now marched off briskly, and about a mile and
a half further on I heard the sound of footsteps in the bush, and,
looking round, as I expected, I spied the craven. . . . Coming up,
his eyes glaring, and his hair bristling on his head, he said, 'It's
all right, the road's clear, and nothing to fear. Come on, I'll give
you a lift; let me carry the swag.' Glad of the relief, throwing
animosity aside, I yielded up the spoil to his care. Sitting down, I
said, 'You go on, I'll have a spell for a bit, and soon overtake
you.'

From the bush I sat in I had a clear view of about three miles of the road from Hartley towards the toll-bar, and past the scene of my late adventure. The first thing I noticed was a long string of men about two hundred yards from that scene, going on the Sydney road from Hartley. This was a gang of prisoners from Bathurst Gaol for Parramatta, guarded by a body of mounted troopers. At the time of my sticking up the mail five or six of these troopers, with the prisoners, were standing in front of the public-house at foot of the hill, about a mile distant.

. . . . I could see a trooper tearing along the road from the direction of the police station at Blackheath, where he had learnt all on the arrival of the coach, and started off in pursuit. Coming to the scene of the disaster he seemed to search carefully around and for some yards into the bush on both sides in quest of the desperado's tracks, but without avail, as he galloped off towards Hartley to raise the hue and cry. The devil was clearly on my side in this transaction, as had it not been for the chain of prisoners requiring the attention of the troopers two of them would have been on the road that morning to meet the mail on Mount Victoria and escort it to the station at Blackheath. . . . Their absence providentially prevented bloodshed.

I must have rested over a quarter of an hour . . . when I started after my mate. In about half a mile further I found, from his tracks in the sandy soil, that he had turned off the track we intended to keep, but being a good hand . . . in running a trail, I easily followed him, and in about a mile more overtook him. 'You're off the track,' I said; 'how's that? . . . You're making on for Bell's line, on the road for Windsor.' . . . I did not dream at that time that the diversion had been made with any treacherous motive. We then partially retraced our steps . . . and reached the hollow at the base of the hill we were making for. I walked up to a large, smooth-barrelled gumtree, and, with my dagger, cut a half moon brand right through the bark into the sap for future guidance. I carried the bag into the centre of a dense thicket . . . secure from espial.

We there emptied the bag, picked out all registered letters and official documents in red tape. . . . Among the first I opened was one containing a publican's cash in three ten-pound notes. Going on with our work, Wilson said, 'Look out particularly for those police letters, there might be something in them that might afterwards seal our doom.' Opening one we found a marked cheque for (I think) £70, drawn by Mr Rouse of Wantagang in favour of one 'S——n'. 'Why,' I said, 'this is the forged cheque for which "S——n" is now awaiting his trial in Bathurst gaol. I know him well; he's not a bad sort of a chap. We'll do him a turn now.' So, after taking out what we thought safe, we burned all the depositions, registered letters, and the cheque; in fact everything connected with the Bathurst cases.

We found a miscellaneous collection of rings, watches, brooches and chains, slices of wedding cake, and a host of (to us) useless articles. Our search over, we found we had about a bucketful of notes, some in halves and some whole. . . . We did not find any corresponding halves, so we put them away with a number of postage stamp sheets, deeming them not negotiable. Gathering up all things we deemed serviceable, we returned them to the mailbag, burying it in a hollow log, and carefully concealing all arms and anything bearing a suspicious look or in any way connected with the robbery. We had now upon us only about a pound's worth of silver, brought from Ironbarks. We made tracks for Bell's line, which joins the Mudgee Road near Brown's mills, Bowenfels.

It was just dark as we went down Brown's Lane on to the Mudgee Road, and this we followed. Having had nothing to eat all day I felt almost knocked up, and proposed making Walton's pub, at the Middle River. I told Wilson we must give our right names to prevent mistakes in future, and pretend that we were just up from Sydney on our way back to the diggings. . . . Before reaching Walton's we came to a small store by the wayside, where I overheard some people talking, and, going to the window, listened. I heard these words, 'What a pity the police have got him arrested, and on his way to Bathurst, on a charge of mail robbery.' This gave me a clue to work on, although I knew nothing of the party alluded to as the culprit. We shortly after pulled up at the public-house. Going in I found that Walton had given up the house. . . . His successor was a retired sergeant of police from Hartley. This looked like running into the lion's mouth, but I trusted to luck and my own ingenuity. I remarked to the new landlord . . . that my name was Bill Day, a gunsmith at Sofala. . . . I told him we would have stopped at Bowenfels, but knowing Walton kept a good house . . . I had pushed on, which accounted for my being so late. A Mr Collis, a squatter, was there at the time, and we each had a drink, and shortly after the landlady came out and sat on a chair near us, sewing.

On the landlord asking me if we came through Hartley, I answered we had. 'Did you hear of the mail robbery?' 'Yes,' said I. 'It was a fearful thing. They have arrested a man at Bowenfels, but I did not hear who he was. It's awful times when a man can't travel the public roads in safety.' 'It's a great loss to me,' said he. 'My £30 for license is gone.'

At this my mate gave me a nudge, which the landlady, I saw, noticed, and a cold shiver ran through me. I knew I must have given him a look like a thundercloud. However, I said to the publican, 'You sort of men ought to keep a good look-out for suspicious-looking tramps.' . . . 'I intend to do so,' he replied; and supper being announced, we went in and sat down, his wife attending on us the while. Nothing could be said between Wilson and myself, but we heartily enjoyed our meal after our long fast.

After supper we re-entered the bar and listened to the general talk, and went early to bed. The landlord asked us if we would breakfast before starting, to which we replied we would, as we were in no hurry. He showed us into the same room I had occupied in my former trips in Walton's time, having a sash window or door opening into the yard.

When I heard his footsteps die away, I turned to my mate and said, 'You foolish wretch, you have done for us by that nudge of yours about the £30. The woman twigged you, as I could tell by her looks that she suspected something.' The night was bitterly cold, with a hard frost. I said, 'I must not go to sleep; I'll go and lie near the fence, on the watch. He's sure to send information about us if she gives him a hint.' I lay there till all the house was in darkness, and hearing or seeing no one on the move, I went back to bed.

We slept in one bed, and Wilson was sound asleep when I came in. We slept till getting on for daybreak, when a tremendous rattling at the bolted door aroused us. 'Who's there?' I cried. 'Police. Open the door.' A constable at once entered and took up his station, pistol in hand, in one corner. When all had entered I was asked, 'Where from?' 'Sydney, but belong to Sofala.' 'Did you come through Hartley, and did you hear of the mail robbery?' 'Yes,' to both. 'Any objection to be searched?' 'No.' On being searched nothing was found on us but a few shillings in silver. Then the first constable said, 'I saw the little man put something under the bedtick while his mate was being searched.' On looking under the mattress, lo and behold! they produced a letter.

I was thunderstruck and gazed on in a daze. They examined the post-offices dates, and found them to correspond with the date of the robbery. It was only a business letter, of no use to us, and what induced Wilson to keep it I could not then understand; but it was done for a purpose, as will be seen. Oh! the treachery of the black-hearted villian. . . . Being satisfied with the letter, the leader of the police said, 'That is all right; we've got them safe now.' We were handcuffed and marched off to Hartley. On the road one constable said to the other beside him, 'It's the little fellow did it; he had the letter.' Wilson heard him.

At Hartley . . . a Mr Denis Gaynor, formerly in the police and a publican on the Turon, though at this time a Bathurst innkeeper, coming forward, said, 'Hilloa! how's this?' Before I could answer the sergeant cried out, 'Let those fifteen go; we've got the right ones this time.' The fifteen roadmen were released. . . . 'Let go No. 16,' came next. The cell door opened, and my companion of the drain on Mount Victoria came forth without any boots on, and loading me with abuse. They had seen the imprints of footmarks in the wet drain, and on examination they tallied with the boots he wore. He had remained in the drain through fright after his companions had gone off, and his not returning with them cast further suspicion on him. In fact, he was adjudged to be the perpetrator of the robbery. . . . The driver of the mail had also been detained to identify and prosecute him. . . .

We were placed in separate cells, and next day Captain Battye came from Bathurst.

Being the first called out, I was taken to the court-house and examined verbally, and bodily for marks (there were plenty of them), and sent back.

Wilson was next called, but what took place I know not. Even then I had but faint suspicion against him. . . . Nothing further occurred for a day or two. One morning I shouted from my cell to my mate; but, receiving no answer, I was puzzled, and my trust in his honesty began to waver. That evening Mr Brown, the police magistrate, and some other gentlemen, came to see me, as a sort of wild beast from a menagerie. On going out, Mr B., being last, placed his hand to the side of his mouth, and said to me, 'He has slewed,' giving me to understand that my mate had turned informer.

I was transfixed with horror. Wilson was led next day to the spot whence we had taken a bird's-eye view of our situation on the first morning of our foray, and pointed out the tree on the hill as being close to the plant of the stolen goods, whither, I suppose, they took him as a guide.

Two days after I was brought for examination, and placed in the dock, before an immense crowd. Seeing my mate coming towards the dock, I made to open the door for him, when Captain Battye said curtly, 'Save yourself the trouble.' Battye prosecuted, saying that Wilson had turned Queen's evidence, and had clearly explained all. He certainly adhered in his evidence strictly to the truth as to our proceedings from the first move. . . . Mr Brown, P.M., then asked me if I had any questions to put to the witness, when I replied, 'No, I think not.' Thereupon I was committed to Bathurst to await my trial, being meantime placed in another cell, and on a chain.

Next morning I was marched off, mounted on a horse (decidedly not a bolter), handcuffed and guarded by two troopers, with the redoubtable captain in true military form in command. In company with us was my recreant mate, also in charge of a constable. I appeared as we passed along like a wild bullock just run in from some outlandish place in the far-away bush. At every public-house on the way our chief and the informer might regale themselves as they listed, but there was no thought for the sufferings of the parched and ferocious bandit, the troopers telling me that they would like to get me a drink, but they dared not. At one place I did get a drink of water. On my telling the captain that some of my own money had been taken from me, and asking if I might not have a glass of ale, he replied, 'Mail money, mail money,' and I went without. That night we reached the Frying Pans, about halfway to Bathurst, where we camped for the night, I being placed in safe keeping, while the informer ate and drank at his ease. The next day was a repetition of the same, and on arrival in Bathurst, the wonder of the day, I was conveyed to the gaol, while Wilson was accommodated in the watchhouse.

For a day or two I was kept on prison rations, and this, with the short allowance daily doled out to me at Hartley, reduced me almost to a state of starvation. In my despair, having dealt largely in my business with Mr Webb, the storekeeper (now the Hon. E. Webb, M.L.C.), I applied to him by letter for some assistance in the shape of food, giving him my name as Bill Day, and saying that I had to wait three months for trial, and if I never paid him God would. To my great joy next day I received a dinner sufficient for two men, with tea and sugar tied up in a cloth. This continued—thanks to his considerate benevolence—till the day of trial.

Years after, going to Bathurst, I met at Cheshire Creek the identical constable who had charge of Wilson on our way from Hartley. I asked him if my mate made any remarks about the affair on the way. 'Oh, yes,' he said, 'he let out that his motive in keeping back the letter was to get you in his power, saying that when he had got you to do the job, he had kept the letter with the intention of hiding it in your place at the Ironbacks, and then telling the police that he and you had been travelling together, that you had given him the slip, and that from your actions he suspected you of having been the party who stuck up the mail. Of course on this information your place would have been overhauled, the letter found, and you lagged. Then he in his own good time would have gone and sprung the plant, and have lived in ease and plenty ever after.' . . .

Some days after, a report was spread in the gaol that Wilson . . . had made his escape from the watchhouse. . . . The lockup-keeper had to attend suddenly on his sick child, and left the door unlocked. Wilson then walked out and was off. . . .

Waiting for trial the time hung heavy on our hands, and to relieve the monotony we instituted a Judge and Jury court, tried one another; and passed sentences, according to statements elicited, which sentences, strange to say, came very near the actual results at the legitimate trials, mine being an exception, as I was awarded at the mock trial fifteen years.

Next day the Assizes were opened, under Judge Dickenson. The Attorney-General (my friend of the mail attack) prosecuted with Mr Lee, Clerk of Arraigns. . . .

The charge being read, I pleaded 'Not Guilty'. The indictment was, 'Stealing from the Postmaster-General a quantity of money and papers, etc.' The Attorney-General then stripped off wig and gown, and stepped into the witness-box, not appearing again in the case, another barrister having taken his place. He (the Attorney-General), having been a passenger by the despoiled coach, swore to my voice, as did also the coachman. The other witnesses against me were Captain Battye and the apprehending constables. The evidence went to show that I was the companion of the 'escaped' informer—who had disclosed the plunder, and who had concealed the Bathurst letter at the inn. This letter was identified by the writer.

The captain had produced the arms with the charges drawn, and was detailing the monies, etc., when the judge requested a statement of the whole amount and not a detailed list. It was given as in gold, money, etc., the amount of £4800. This evidence was quite sufficient to convict me.

It appeared in the course of investigation that the landlord at Middle River, after turning out the lights, had slipped off unseen by me and given the information leading to our arrest, for which he received the £100 reward.

I was then called on for my defence, but having no witnesses I produced certificates of character from the highest and most influential men on the western goldfields, including the Commissioners and J.Ps. I addressed the jury for about an hour and a half. I injured myself, although it may not have had any effect on the result. When the acting Attorney-General rose to reply I appealed to the judge as to whether it was usual when a prisoner was undefended for the Attorney-General to use his right of reply. On this knowing hit the acting Attorney-General resumed his seat, and the jury retired.

In the absence of the jury, the court being quite quiet, the judge went to his room. There was a man standing by my wife, who was present in the body of the court, who asked me how I thought to get on. I replied, 'Sure to be found guilty, and likely to receive ten years, with about three years in irons.'

The Attorney-General himself, who was sitting close in front of me, cast an eye of wonder on me, but did not speak. After about an hour the jury returned into court with a verdict of 'Guilty'. I made a long appeal to the judge on behalf of my wife and family; but a deaf ear was turned to me.

The judge, in passing sentence, remarked that as the robbery had not been committed through want, his determination was to give me the utmost penalty the law provided. In the course of his speech, knowing I could not make matters worse, I frequently interrupted him, but was met with a stern, 'Silence, prisoner.' 'There was one thing,' he said, 'instead of being indicted for stealing you ought to have been arraigned on a charge of highway robbery under arms, and the Attorney-General might now withdraw the one and substitute the other charge.' To this the Attorney-General did not assent. The judge continued, 'Under the latter charge it would have lain in my power to give you imprisonment for life, while the highest sentence on the former is seven years, which I now inflict on you, with hard labour on the public works of the colony.'

NORMAN A. RICHARDSON

Pioneer Mailmen of South Australia

From The Pioneers of the North-West of South Australia, 1856 to 1914, *(Adelaide, 1925; Facsimile edition published by the State Library of South Australia, 1969).*

————————

Previous to 1876 the residents of the country north-west of Port Augusta [South Australia] were dependent upon one another to get their mail matter from Port Augusta, and sometimes weeks passed without any news from the outside world. The Euro Bluff people used to send a man on horseback once a fortnight to Narcoona (Mortlock's station), on the western plain, 25 miles distant, to get the mail. As the only track to the north-west went via this station all letters and papers for people out beyond would lie there until some passing traveller took them on. In June, 1875, a public meeting was held at Euro Bluff for the purpose of endeavouring to obtain a regular mail service. . . At that meeting it was resolved to enlist the services of the member for the district (Patrick Boyce Coglin) to assist in securing a regular mail service to The Elizabeth Creek, 120 miles from Port Augusta, and as a result of his efforts tenders were called for a fortnightly service. Norman Richardson was the successful tenderer. The route was via Euro Bluff (first stage of 35 miles), thence via Whittata (30 miles, but no permanent water) to Pernatty Station, 20 miles farther on, where there was permanent water, which place had to be reached before a fresh team could be obtained. This stage was a hard one to get over, especially in a droughty season.

From Euro Bluff to Pernatty was 50 miles of heavy road, with big sandhills at both ends.

From Pernatty the next stage was to The Elizabeth, via Yeltacowie, a distance of 25 miles. On the last Saturday in March, 1876, the first mail was dispatched, and George West (a well-known identity of those days) carried it on horseback. The contents of that first terminal bag contained four newspapers—three Observers and another weekly—and three letters, and John Macdonald, who was at that time manager of The Elizabeth Station, was the first postmaster in the north-west. All the stations along the route had their own private bags, which the mailman had to deliver, and for this they paid the Postal Department £2 a year.

Although this contract had been let as a horseback service, Richardson immediately put on a light conveyance and carried passengers. It was a very sandy, heavy track, and the most of the way through thick mulga and myall scrub, and the Pernatty sandhills were·particularly steep and heavy. The only road or track was that which had been made by the wheels of some heavily-loaded waggons. To avoid this heavy track, the mailman used frequently to strike out a new one for himself. This he invariably did through the thickest scrub he could find, so as, if possible, to prevent the teamsters following him with their waggons. Mrs John Macdonald, who still (1925) resides in Port Augusta, was the first passenger on this line. It was a usual custom for the coach passengers to alight at the foot of a high sandhill and walk up to the top, in order to relieve the tired horses. On one occasion the coach going up was heavily laden. Most of the passengers were station hands, but one was the manager of a large station—an autocrat. Driver Tommy Maloney said, 'I'll thank you, gentlemen, to walk to the top.' All except the manager promptly alighted; but 'Mr Manager' said, 'No, I'm damned if I do; I've paid my fare, and I'm going to ride.' 'All right, sir,' said the driver. He immediately took the hobbles out of the coach and put them on his horses and commenced to unharness them. 'What the devil are you doing?' demanded 'Mr Manager.' 'Oh, we will turn out and camp here until the morning, sir; the horses will be fresh to get over the hill then,' replied Maloney. 'Damnation!' ejaculated the manager, and with a jump and six hasty strides he was over the hill, and the coach soon followed him.

From Euro Bluff to Port Augusta West was a stage of 35 miles, most of the way through thickly-timbered country, and no water between places. It was the usual custom to hobble the horses out for a roll and a feed in the middle of the day, and to boil the billy under the spreading myall-tree. On one occasion, among the passengers on the coach was a manager's wife and her little girl, some three years old. Close alongside the camping-place the native peach trees grew in great profusion, and were loaded with ripe red fruit. During dinner-time the little girl, unnoticed, wandered away, looking for the pretty red fruit, and when the coach was ready for starting she was missing. In spite of a vigorous search she could not be found, and the distressed parent had to come on by the coach to the Port without her child. It was late at night when the coach reached the Port. A search party, including the child's father, was soon formed, and immediately proceeded to the spot where the child had been lost. At daylight, after a little delay, the wee tracks were discovered and rapidly followed. Eventually they came to a bush under which the little wanderer had evidently slept for some hours. With the trackers spread out, right and left, they pushed on, and at length, at the edge of an open patch of country, the figure of the child was discerned, and a rush was made for her. The child, upon seeing her father, ran up to him and exclaimed, 'Daddy, Mummy went away and left me.' The little wanderer had traversed about eight miles of thick scrub, and was none the worse for the outing. . .

*　　　*　　　*

In the early 'eighties, when squatters were commencing to fence their country, the mailman had made a short cut through the scrub to avoid the teamsters' track, which was much cut up and in consequence very heavy for light vehicles. This track was about half-way between Euro Bluff and Whittata. Going up one week the driver found a new six-wire fence across his track. He cut it, went through, loosely did up the wires, and proceeded on his way. Upon his return trip he found that the fence had been mended. He repeated his previous performance. Next week he again found the fence properly repaired, and again he cut it. On his return trip as he came in sight of the fence he discerned a man standing on the road, a big dog behind him and a gun leaning on the fence at his side. The driver remarked to his passengers, 'There is a row on here.' It was a smoking-hot day. Pulling up, he saluted the stranger with, 'Good day; very hot!' 'Yes, it is hot,' replied the man at the fence. 'Do you care for a nobbler?' queried the driver. 'Thanks, yes!' was the reply, and scrambling through the fence he came to the side of the coach, enjoyed his nip, and discussed the weather. 'Well, I must be getting along,' remarked the driver. 'Wait a bit,' said the other, 'I'll open the fence for you.' The row was averted, and next trip the driver found a nice handy gate put there. Moral—'Discretion is the better part of valour.'

BILL WANNAN

Who's Robbing this Coach?

There are certain phrases that have become part and parcel of the Australian idiom and are hardly likely to go out of fashion in the forseeable future.

'You haven't got Buckley's' (you haven't got a chance), 'Sydney or the bush' (all or nothing), and 'Send 'er down, Hughie!' (let the rain fall down in torrents!) come readily to mind.

One typically Australian expression which used to puzzle me a little is the old familiar 'Who's robbing this coach?' What does it mean exactly? Does it imply that the person thus addressed should mind his own business? Or does it mean, in effect, 'Who's in charge around here—me or you?'

An old and enduring anecdote, very widely known in Australia, throws light on the probable origin of this phrase. It would suggest that the meaning is, indeed, 'Mind your own business!'

One day, so the story goes, Ned Kelly stuck up a mail coach and ordered all the passengers to alight and line themselves up in a row.

When they had done this, the notorious outlaw announced, 'Now I'm going to rob all the men and kiss all the ladies!'

A gallant young fellow promptly shouted, 'You scoundrel! Leave the women alone!'

A middle-aged spinster in the line-up broke in with: 'You mind your own business, young man! Who's robbing this coach—you or Mr Kelly?

'J. J. G. BRADLEY' (JAMES SKIPP BORLASE)
How Ned Kelly Met Lola Montez

Ned Kelly, the outlaw, had become a folk hero before his death by hanging at the Melbourne Jail in November 1880. His career as a bushranger was largely concurrent with those of Jesse James and Billy the Kid. Like them Kelly became a legend in his lifetime, and a figure whose heroic proportions have (whether rightly or wrongly) grown with the years. Potboiling writers were quick to see the ingredients of romantic adventure in Ned Kelly's bushranging exploits. In 1881 a London printer put out a serial in regular parts, Ned Kelly The Ironclad Australian Bushranger, *a 'penny blood' thriller in which the anonymous author let his imagination run riot. The following account of a meeting between the outlaw and Lola Montez the dancer is typical. Actually, Ned was only seven years old when Lola Montez died in 1861. The story is known to be the work of James Borlase, who wrote under various pseudonyms: 'J. J. G. Bradley', 'Skip Borlase', and 'Captain Leslie'; and who contributed many 'penny bloods' for boys' journals and other publications. I included the excerpt that follows in my collection,* A Treasury of Australian Frontier Tales; *and as that anthology has long been out of print, and is not likely to be revived, I felt that the Ned Kelly-Lola Montez episode was worthy of resuscitation in the present miscellany.*

———————

How bright that full, large, fair Australian moon is! The smallest print could be read beneath its rays. It floods hill and plain, bush and scrub, with its soft white light, and all the creatures that love the night are up and about to enjoy it.

The locusts drone like bagpipes out of tune in the tree branches, and the low, plaintive note of the mopoke, or Australian cuckoo, is answered by the still more mournful cry of wild fowl from some neighbouring swamp, or the howl of the warrigal, or wild dog, from the deepest recesses of the bush.

But all these sounds together are eclipsed in mournfulness by the rattling of the loose bark against the tree-trunks, which, where their last year's clothing has fallen off, gleam as white as sheeted ghosts on all sides.

Is this a wonderful constellation, or a comet, coming rushing through the trees with the speed of the very wind?

No, it is three great lamps marking the three points of a triangle.

As it approaches nearer a vehicle all ablaze with scarlet and gold, and in shape not unlike a circus band carriage, may be descried, drawn by four long, weedy-looking horses that have the go of the very devil in them.

High up on the raised box sits a tall, slab-sided Yankee, wearing a soft drab felt hat, at least a yard in height from the brim, which is almost wide enough to hold a donkey race on; in his left hand he holds a fistfull of reins, and in his right grasps a whip 15 feet long in the lash, with which he can flick a fly from off one of the leaders' ears, or give a crack as loud as any rifle shot.

But where the deuce is the man driving? Well may that question be asked, for to the uninitiated there is not a trace of a road visible.

No it is all grassy bush; ups and downs, bumps and hollows, felled trees and standing trees, bushes and huge scattered pieces of bark.

But this is Cobb's royal mail coach, doing its 609 miles between Melbourne and Sydney, and there isn't one of Cobb's drivers who would hesitate to take his gaudy, springless, wide-wheeled and wholly uncomfortable vehicle over the ruts of an earthquake or down the sides of Mont Blanc, if told by his employers that the thing had to be done.

When the enterprising Cobb first started his Yankee coaches in Australia he had to battle against some opposition, but proffering to convey the Government mails to Ballarat three hours quicker than any other coach proprietor, he was given the chance of doing so.

Most people like fast travelling and so the new Yankee coach was crowded the first day of its run, but it didn't arrive so at the end of its journey. At first it was all very delightful, but when the metal had been left behind (it didn't extend very far in those days), and the driver evinced a decided inclination to reach his destination much as the crow flies—that is to say, on the bee-line principle, with a contemptuous disdain for all intervening obstacles—even the bravest began to feel nervous, if not absolutely terrified.

Matters grew worse and worse. First one side of the coach would fly up in the air and then the other. Next it would be plunging like a ship in a rough sea, and anon seem as though it was contemplating turning a complete summersault.

'For goodness sake be careful!'

Such and many a similar petition was hurled at the driver's ears by the passengers, who every minute were being shaken together, or almost pitched over the sides; but the tall-hatted Jehu paid not the slightest attention to their remonstrances or prayers, so they at last began to let themselves down over the back, an easy feat enough, and anyhow better than remaining where they were to be pitched out and killed.

Suffice it to say Cobb's coach reached its destination without a single passenger aboard, but it won the mail contract, and has kept it ever since, and now hundreds of its coaches and thousands of its horses traverse the four leading colonies of Australia in every direction. People soon took to travelling by them when they discovered that accidents seldom or never occurred—indeed, they are so wide between the wheels that, with the entire absence of top-hamper, there is little chance of a capsize, except through a wheel coming off.

But to return to our story.

On comes the particular coach with which we have to deal, the wheels now and then almost shaving a gum-tree trunk, or the end of a felled sheaoak, as it whizzes along through the moonlit bush.

The driver might have followed the new road had he liked, but he prefers the old route; all the more as the bush track does not knock his horses' feet to pieces like metal.

Suddenly a dark and mysterious form spurs a big bay horse out from amongst a neighbouring clump of trees, and plants himself directly in the coach's track.

Cries of alarm ring forth from inside the vehicle, and a passenger who produces a brace of pistols has them forcibly wrested from him and thrown away: for everyone seems to know by instinct that that ill-omened vision in front of them is a bushranger, and the passengers, almost without an exception, are fearful that the least opposition may anger the outlaw into butchering them all in cold blood.

'Bail up, you——!' (both adjective and substantive are too blasphemous and disgusting to be printed). 'Bail up, or I'll put an ounce of lead through your brain-pan!' shouts the stranger to the driver, as he draws a pistol from his holster.

'All right, sirree. Job Fairweather's always ready to yield a convincing argument such as that there!' rejoins the Yankee, coolly; and reining up his cattle he proceeds to light a big cigar.

The man on horseback now rides slowly up to the coach, and, as he draws near, the terrified passengers observe his strange iron head-dress and cuirass.

'It's the ironclad bushranger himself,' whispers one in quavering tones.

'Yes, it's that infernal rascal, Kelly, without doubt,' echoes another.

'Up with your hands above your heads, every man Jack of you. Up with them, I say. By thunder, I'll brain the man who disobeys my orders. Your pardon, ladies, don't be alarmed, *your* sex protects you from harm, but I must have your watches and other jewellery as souvenirs of your charms. Hullo, you with the white choker—I like a parson for an assistant—just empty those fellows' pockets of their contents and hand them to me.'

'My good man, respect my cloth,' pleaded the clergyman, very meekly.

'You are a lying hound, notwithstanding your cloth, to call me a good man, when you know well that I'm about the biggest villain left unhung. Do as I bid you, or you'll never patter from a pulpit again. Turn each pocket inside out that I may be sure you aren't tricking me, and if you find anything of an explosive nature in either of them don't by accident turn it this way, or by similar accident the contents of my pistol will get mixed up with your brains. A wink's as good as a nod to a blind horse, you know.'

'But, I—I'm not a horse,' faltered the hesitating divine.

'Well, perhaps *ass* would be nearer the mark, in your case, and had I an ass that wouldn't go, wouldn't I pistol him? By heaven, don't force me to finish the couplet, or I'll end it in d—— unpleasant pantomime;' and as he concluded he thrust the muzzle of his weapon within a couple of inches of the clergyman's head, who thereupon yielded to the exigencies of the position.

'I *must* turn pickpocket, gentlemen,' said he plaintively. 'It's a great disgrace to my cloth; but necessity has no law. Pray allow me!' and he proceeded to do his work effectively and well, now and then exclaiming in muffled monotone, 'For God's sake, gentlemen, continue to keep your hands up in the air, or the miscreant will murder us all in cold blood. Do, there's good fellows.'

The 'good fellows' did exactly as they were told, for they had quite as much objection to being shot at, as had the clergyman himself.

When all their valuables had been transferred to the ironclad bushranger's pockets, and every one of their own had been turned inside out, Ned Kelly turned to the womenkind, of whom there were three aboard the coach, and said—

'Now, ladies, I can hardly set the parson to search *you*, for I daresay the black cloth that he prides himself on would blush as scarlet as a soldier's coat at the mere thought of such a thing. I trust to your honour, therefore, to give me all that you have about you. Chains and watches I know all of you possess, and rings on your fingers as well. Stay, up with your veils in the first place. Ned Kelly don't often look upon a woman's face.'

Up went two of the veils at once. The third fair one hesitated.

'The really beautiful are always modest,' said the daring outlaw. 'Madam, I have heard that you are partial to kings; won't you show your face to the Ironclad King of the Australian bush?'

'Ah! you know me!' exclaimed the veiled female, in a slightly foreign accent. 'Well, if you want very much to see my face, there!'

And so saying, with two of the tiniest hands, she raised her veil, and revealed a countenance in every way calculated to enthral even the most impressionless by its rich, flowing voluptuous Southern beauty.

No twin stars that gleamed down from out the indigo-hued heavens were as bright as those large, dark, melting orbs, which, however, seemed to be equally full of fire.

They were shaded by the longest and silkiest of curved lashes, and surmounted by the most beautifully-arched of jetty brows.

Her hair was brushed back from a low, broad forehead, white and pure as snow. Her features were most delicately chiselled, her rich, full lips were red and pouting, her chin disarmingly dimpled, her full, rounded throat as fair as alabaster. She looked a prize worthy indeed of a monarch.

By this time the other women had handed to the bushranger all their valuables, but he took them mechanically, and all the while was seemingly unable to avert his gaze from the enchantress's face.

'Lola Montez, Countess of Lansfeldt,' said he, 'your destiny is to become the wife of Ned Kelly, the King of the Australian bush. The parson shall marry us at once, and then I'll take you right away to your future home in the mountain ranges. What do you say to my plan, Countess?'

'That I haven't so much as seen your face. How can I tell whether I shall like you? I have shown you mine; 'tis but fair that I should behold yours in return.'

'Well, I don't know but what it is.' And the bushranger dropped his reins on his horse's neck, and raised his ponderous iron head-dress.

Hardly had he done so, however, when the beautiful woman (we have her portrait before us whilst we write) pulled a small pistol from within her sleeve and fired it point-blank at the bushranger's face, accompanying the action with the contemptuous remark—

'Where seven men sink panic-stricken before a single villain, 'tis time for a woman to show what she can do.'

Unfortunately, the beautiful specimen of the sex in question had not done nearly so much as she intended.

The little bullet from her almost toy weapon, instead of penetrating to the bushranger's brain, had only shorn off a portion of his left ear.

Maddened by pain and rage, he hastily redonned his helmet, and, dashing up to the coach side, hissed between his teeth—

'For that act of treachery I won't marry you at all. Lola Montez, Countess of Lansfeldt, and sometime almost Queen of Bavaria, shall become the mate instead of the wife of the King of the Australian Bush. Come, quit that d——coach for the crupper of my horse on the instant, ere I force you to obey me with a grip on one of those plump arms that'll leave a livid ring for weeks.'

'Ruffian, you shall kill me before I will consent to go with you!'

'By heaven, but you *shall* go with me. Now, you men, keep up those hands, and at the same time keep still. I don't want to ruin the ladies' dresses with the blood and brains of any of you, so take care that you don't drive me to it. If you stroke my fur the wrong way by daring to interfere on this woman's behalf, I'll slaughter the whole biling of you in cold blood, by George I will. Now, Madam, look lively. I've taken an oath to have you, and by thunder I will, so make no more to do about it.'

He spurred his horse still closer alongside the coach as he spoke, and grasped her by an arm, but no sooner had he done so than his hand was slashed across by the keen blade of an Albacete knife.

'Tiger cat!' he yelled, as he let go his clutch, 'throw that knife away, or I'll put a bullet through you, beautiful as an angel though you are.'

'Do it, ruffian. Better death than to fall alive into the power of such as you.'

Whether Ned Kelly would have shot her, or whether he used the threat merely to intimidate the proud and courageous Spanish beauty into yielding to his will, is a point that has never been decided, for at this critical and highly dramatic position of affairs another pistol rang out, and Ned Kelly wheeled his horse round to confront four well-mounted men, the foremost of whom held his smoking weapon still in his grasp.

'Sheer off, my hearties, unless you want me to give you a swift journey to purgatory,' exclaimed Ned Kelly with an oath. 'I don't suppose you guessed who I was, only seeing my back, eh?'

He spoke in sneering accents, but then all in an instant his tone altered to a shriek of vindictive and triumphant rage.

'Squatter M'Pherson as I live! And so the devil at last has delivered you into my hands? Take this from the lover of the girl you murdered, whom you left to die of want in the bush, you smock-faced scoundrel.'

As he spoke, he transferred his reins to his teeth, and drawing his pistols from his holsters, fired both point blank at the squatter.

It was very seldom that Ned Kelly's bullets didn't fly true to their billets, and he was, as a rule, equally handy with his left hand as his right; but on the present occasion the rage and excitement under which he laboured caused both balls to fly wide, and the next instant two of those who were with the squatter fired at the bushranger in turn, and he found to his dismay and chagrin that a ball had penetrated his right shoulder, depriving him of all use in that arm, whilst he was more than suspicious, from its rearing, that the other had wounded his horse.

Not to flee for his very life under such adverse circumstances would have been little short of madness, so, setting spurs to the troop horse, Ned Kelly broke through the four mounted men, who in vain endeavoured to lay hands upon him as he passed, and made off into the bush.

JOHN SADLEIR

'A Very Remarkable Feat'

From Recollections of a Victorian Police Officer *(Melbourne, 1913). Sadleir (1833–1919) was an officer and subsequently an Inspecting-Superintendent of Police in Victoria during a turbulent frontier period, being closely concerned with the capture of Ned Kelly in 1880.*

―――――――

When I arrived at Hamilton, Victoria, in 1859 there were no coaches nor other regular means of communication with Melbourne, or the coastal towns, Port Fairy and Portland. It was due to the enterprise of Cobb & Co., or some other Yankee or Canadian association, that the first coaches were put on the road connecting Hamilton with these places. If I remember aright, the first line of coaches was from Portland through Hamilton, Wickliffe and Ararat, and thence to Geelong and Melbourne. A later route turned east at Wickliffe, reaching Geelong *via* Streatham, Lismore and Rokewood. Still later when the railway to Ballarat was completed the route from Wickliffe was through Skipton, Lintons, Smythesdale to Ballarat and thence by rail to Melbourne. Portland continued to be the coastal terminus of all these routes, as it was also the last port of call for the steamers plying westward along the coast. Indeed, Portland might be considered as the only port, for in 1859 Warrnambool had not come into any prominence, and Port Fairy, then known as Belfast, was in a state of decay, the grass growing over its empty streets. One driver named Miles drove the stage between Portland and Wickliffe daily, a very remarkable feat, considering that he must have often sat on the box for 12 to 14 hours. It was said that he slept on the stage over the plain from Wickliffe to

Dunkeld, and had forty winks before reaching Hamilton. I have seen Miles half an hour after his arrival at Portland, adorned with gold chain and numerous ornaments, fresh and dainty as if he had stepped out of a bandbox. He was supposed to be wooing the landlady of Mac's Hotel.

JOHN SADLEIR

A Dangerous Road

From Recollections of a Victorian Police Officer *(Melbourne, 1913)*.

—————————

In the early 'sixties when gold was discovered at Woods' Point, Vic., an attempt was made to use what is still called the Yarra track, as the line of communication between Melbourne and the new goldfield. This track, after reaching Marysville, commenced the ascent to the summit of a spur that continued at a moderately even level until it joined the main divide at Matlock. The first six miles, from Marysville to Tommy's Bend, led up a steep and continuous incline, and over this portion the Government had constructed a well-formed metal road, while the remaining 40 or 50 miles were simply cleared of timber. But the road was never found quite practicable. The summit of the spur was composed of deep rich soil, which practically never dried—in its least sodden state, the 'glue-pot' stage, it was at its worst—and there were so many accidents and delays that its use for general traffic was abandoned. Cobb & Co., with their usual enterprise, had put a line of coaches, but this, too, was given up when one of their coaches with its team of horses fell into a ravine, and met with a grievous smash. The leaders shied at an old lady in a bright red cloak, as she sat by the roadside waiting to take her place in the coach, and dragged the other horses and coach into the gully.

Even the metalled road at the Marysville end had its dangers, as I learned by personal experience in the descent from Tommy's Bend. In spite of a powerful brake, twice I was compelled to run the horses and trap into the bank on the upper side to avoid disaster. I suppose even to this day [1913] there may be found, all over the unmade parts of the Yarra track, the wreckage of vehicles that became fixed in the deep mud, or were overwhelmed in the winter snows and were left derelict.

K. A. AUSTIN

'Let 'er Go, Gallagher!'

From The Lights of Cobb and Co.: The Story of the Frontier Coaches, *1854–1924 (Seal Books edition, Adelaide, 1972).*

Perhaps the best remembered of all Cobb & Co.'s Road Managers was Tom Gallagher. In 1881, when he and his brother, John, were operating the mail service between St George and Thargomindah in south-western Queensland, their line was amalgamated with Cobb & Co. Tom was noted as a vigorous driver, and the saying 'Let her go, Gallagher,' meaning something like 'step on it,' was a popular expression as late as the 1920s. Rutherford soon made him a Road Manager. He played a great part in the development of Cobb & Co.'s services in Queensland, and in the process acquired an impressive detailed knowledge of conditions along all the Company's routes, which he never forgot, for his memory was remarkable. Mr F. P. Archer, who knew Gallagher before the first World War, gives this description of him:

'I recall Tom Gallagher as a tall spare man, with a clipped and pointed beard, dour and silent mostly, a great man to stand up for his drivers—but he expected them to look after their teams and to "study the interests of the Company." He was a wonderful judge of horses, with a great memory for them—recalling where this and that one were in certain teams on his previous visit to the district—the bay horse in the middle lead or the roan horse in the off-side wheel, etc. The drivers had a great respect for him in every way, and good drivers worked under him for years.

One thing about Tom Gallagher was the way he would walk

round the teams to see if they had cattle blight, or 'blue eye', and he always said to use Champion's vinegar, squirted into the eye, as a treatment. It was generally referred to as "Cobb & Co. treatment," or "Cobb's Remedy" '.

The Shanty-keeper's Wife

Henry Lawson (1867–1922) wrote four short stories dealing directly with stage-coaching—drivers, passengers, and the facilities at the stages. They are all included in this miscellany. 'The Shanty-keeper's Wife' and 'The Exciseman' are masterpieces of Lawson's storytelling art. But each of the four illustrates the knowledge of his subject-matter and the authenticity of his characters and backgrounds, which are so much a part of his greatness as a writer.

'The Shanty-keeper's Wife' is from the collection, Over the Sliprails *(Sydney, 1900).*

There were about a dozen of us jammed into the coach, on the box seat and hanging on to the roof and tailboard as best we could. We were shearers, bagmen, agents, a squatter, a cockatoo, the usual joker—and one or two professional spielers, perhaps. We were tired and stiff and nearly frozen—too cold to talk and too irritable to risk the inevitable argument which an interchange of ideas would have led up to. We had been looking forward for hours, it seemed, to the pub where we were to change horses. For the last hour or two all that our united efforts had been able to get out of the driver was a grunt to the effect that it was ''bout a couple o'miles'. Then he said, or grunted, ''Tain't fur now,' a couple of times, and refused to commit himself any further; he seemed grumpy about having committed himself so far.

He was one of those men who take everything in dead earnest; who regard any expression of ideas outside their own sphere of life as trivial, or, indeed, if addressed directly to them, as offensive;

who, in fact, are darkly suspicious of anything in the shape of a joke or laugh on the part of an outsider in their own particular dust-hole. He seemed to be always thinking, and thinking a lot; when his hands were not both engaged, he would tilt his hat forward and scratch the base of his skull with his little finger, and let his jaw hang. But his intellectual powers were mostly concentrated on a doubtful swingle-tree, a misfitting collar, or that there bay or piebald (on the off or near side) with the sore shoulder.

Casual letters or papers, to be delivered on the road, were matters which troubled him vaguely, but constantly—like the abstract ideas of his passengers.

The joker of our party was a humorist of the dry order, and had been slyly taking rises out of the driver for the last two or three stages. But the driver only brooded. He wasn't the one to tell you straight if you offended him, or if he fancied you offended him, and thus gain your respect, or prevent a misunderstanding which would result in life-long enmity. He might meet you in after years when you had forgotten all about your trespass—if indeed you had ever been conscious of it—and 'stoush' you unexpectedly on the ear.

Also you might regard him as your friend, on occasion, and yet he would stand by and hear a perfect stranger tell you the most outrageous lies, to your hurt, and know that the stranger was telling lies, and never put you up to it. It would never enter his head to do so. It wouldn't be any affair of his—only an abstract question.

It grew darker and colder. The rain came as if the frozen south were spitting at our face and neck and hands, and our feet grew as big as camels', and went dead, and we might as well have stamped the footboards with wooden legs for all the feeling we got into our own. But they were more comfortable that way, for the toes didn't curl up and pain so much, nor did our corns stick out so hard against the leather, and shoot.

We looked out eagerly for some clearing, or fence, or light— some sign of the shanty where we were to change horses—but there was nothing save blackness all round. The long, straight, cleared road was no longer relieved by the ghostly patch of light, far ahead, where the bordering tree-walls came together in perspective and framed the ether. We were down in the bed of the bush.

We pictured a haven of rest with a suspended lamp burning in the frosty air outside and a big log fire in a cosy parlour off the bar, and a long table set for supper. But this is a land of contradictions; wayside shanties turn up unexpectedly, and in the most unreasonable places, and are, as likely as not, prepared for a banquet when you are not hungry and can't wait, and as cold and dark as a bushman's grave when you are and can.

Suddenly the driver said: 'We're there.' He said this as if he had driven us to the scaffold to be hanged, and was fiercely glad that he'd got us there safely at last. We looked but saw nothing; then a light appeared ahead and seemed to come towards us; and presently we saw that it was a lantern held up by a man in a slouch hat, with a dark bushy beard, and a three-bushel bag around his shoulders. He held up his other hand, and said something to the driver in a tone that might have been used by the leader of a search party who had just found the body. The driver stopped and then went on slowly.

'What's up? we asked. 'What's the trouble?'

'Oh, it's all right,' said the driver.

'The publican's wife is sick,' somebody said, 'and he wants us to come quietly.'

The usual little slab-and-bark shanty was suggested in the gloom, with a big bark stable looming in the background. We climbed down like so many cripples. As soon as we began to feel our legs and be sure we had the right ones and the proper allowance of feet, we helped, as quietly as possible, to take the horses out and round to the stable.

'Is she very bad?' we asked the publican, showing as much concern as we could.

'Yes,' he said, in the subdued voice of a rough man who had spent several anxious, sleepless nights by the sick-bed of a dear one. 'But, God willing, I think we'll pull her through.'

Thus encouraged we said, sympathetically: 'We're very sorry to trouble you, but I suppose we could manage to get a drink and a bit to eat?'

'Well,' he said, 'there's nothing to eat in the house, and I've only got rum and milk. You can have that if you like.'

One of the pilgrims broke out here.

'Well, of all the pubs,' he began, 'that I've ever—'

'Hush-sh-sh!' said the publican.

The pilgrim scowled and retired to the rear. You can't express your feelings freely when there's a woman dying close handy.

'Well, who says rum and milk?' asked the joker in a low voice.

'Wait here,' said the publican, and disappeared into the little front passage.

Presently a light showed through a window with a scratched and fly-bitten B and A on two panes, and a mutilated R on the third, which was broken. A door opened, and we sneaked into the bar. It was like having drinks after hours where the police are strict and independent.

When we came out the driver was scratching his head and looking at the harness on the veranda floor.

'You fellows'll have ter put in the time for an hour or so. The horses is out back somewheres,' and he indicated the interior of Australia with a side jerk of his head, 'and the boy ain't back with 'em yet.'

'But dash it all,' said the pilgrim, 'me and my mate——'

'Hush!' said the publican.

'How long are the horses likely to be?' we asked the driver.

'Dunno,' he grunted. 'Might be three or four hours. It's all accordin'.'

'Now, look here,' said the pilgrim, 'me and my mate wanter catch the train.'

'Hush-sh-sh!' from the publican in a fierce whisper.

'Well, boss,' said the joker, 'can you let us have beds, then? I don't want to freeze here all night, anyway.'

'Yes,' said the landlord, 'I can do that, but some of you will have to sleep double and some of you'll have to take it out of the sofas, and one or two'll have to make a shake-down on the floor. There's plenty of bags in the stable, and you've got rugs and coats with you. Fix it up amongst yourselves.'

'But look here!' interrupted the pilgrim, desperately, 'we can't afford to wait! We're only "battlers," me and my mate, pickin' up crumbs by the wayside. We've got to catch the——'

'Hush!' said the publican, savagely. 'You fool, didn't I tell you my missus was bad? I won't have any noise.'

'But look here,' protested the pilgrim, 'we must catch the train at Dead Camel——'

'You'll catch my boot presently,' said the publican, with a savage oath, 'and go further than Dead Camel. I won't have my missus disturbed for you or any other man! Just you shut up or get out, and take your blooming mate with you.'

We lost patience with the pilgrim and sternly took him aside.

'Now, for God's sake, hold your jaw,' we said. 'Haven't you got any consideration at all? Can't you see the man's wife is ill—dying perhaps—and he nearly worried off his head?'

The pilgrim and his mate were scraggy little bipeds of the city push variety, so they were suppressed.

'Well,' yawned the joker, 'I'm not going to roost on a stump all night. I'm going to turn in.'

'It'll be eighteenpence each,' hinted the landlord. 'You can settle now if you like to save time.'

We took the hint, and had another drink. I don't know how we 'fixed it up amongst ourselves,' but we got settled down somehow. There was a lot of mysterious whispering and scuffling round by the light of a couple of dirty greasy bits of candle. Fortunately we dared not speak loud enough to have a row, though most of us were by this time in the humour to pick a quarrel with a long-lost brother.

The joker got the best bed, as good-humoured, good-natured chaps generally do, without seeming to try for it. The growler of the party got the floor and chaff-bags, as selfish men mostly do—without seeming to try for it either. I took it out of one of the 'sofas,' or rather that sofa took it out of me. It was short and narrow and down by the head, with a leaning to one corner on the outside, and had more nails and bits of gin-case than original sofa in it.

I had been asleep for three seconds, it seemed, when somebody shook me by the shoulder and said:

'Take yer seats.'

When I got out, the driver was on the box, and the others were getting rum and milk inside themselves (and in bottles) before taking their seats.

It was colder and darker than ever and the South Pole seemed nearer; and pretty soon, but for the rum, we should have been in a worse fix than before.

There was a spell of grumbling. Presently someone said:

'I don't believe them horses was lost at all. I was round behind the stable before I went to bed, and seen horses there; and if they wasn't them same horses there, I'll eat 'em raw!'

'Would yer?' said the driver, in a disinterested tone.

'I would,' said the passanger. Then, with a sudden ferocity, 'and you too!'

The driver said nothing. It was an abstract question which didn't interest him.

We saw that we were on delicate ground, and changed the subject for a while. Then someone else said:

'I wonder where his missus was? I didn't see any signs of her about, or any other woman about the place, and we was pretty well all over it.'

'Must have kept her in the stable,' suggested the joker.

'No, she wasn't, for Scotty and that chap on the roof was there after bags.'

'She might have been in the loft,' reflected the joker.

'There was no loft,' put in a voice from the top of the coach.

'I say, Mister—Mister man,' said the joker suddenly to the driver, 'Was his missus sick at all?'

'I dunno,' replied the driver. 'She might have been. He said so, anyway. I ain't got no call to call a man a liar.'

'See here,' said the cannibalistic individual to the driver, in the tone of a man who has made up his mind for a row, 'has that shanty-keeper got a wife at all?'

'I believe he has.'

'And is she living with him?'

'No, she ain't—if yer wanter know.'

'Then where is she?'

'I dunno. How am I to know? She left him three or four years ago. She was in Sydney last time I heard of her. It ain't no affair of mine, anyways.'

'And is there any woman about the place at all, driver?' inquired a professional wanderer reflectively.

'No—not that I knows of. There useter be an old black gin come pottering round sometimes, but I ain't seen her lately.'

'And excuse me, driver, but is there anyone round there at all?' inquired the professional wanderer, with the air of a conscientious writer, collecting material for an Australian novel from life, and with an eye to detail.

'Naw,' said the driver—and recollecting that he was expected to be civil and obliging to his employers' patrons, he added in surly apology, 'Only the boss and the stableman, that I knows of.' Then repenting of the apology, he asserted his manhood again, and asked, in a tone calculated to risk a breach of the peace, 'Any more questions, gentlemen—while the shop's open?'

There was a long pause.

'Driver,' asked the pilgrim appealingly, 'was them horses lost at all?'

'I dunno,' said the driver. 'He said they was. He's got the looking after them. It was nothing to do with me.'

'Twelve drinks at sixpence a drink'—said the joker, as if calculating to himself—'that's six bob, and, say on an average, four shouts—that's one pound four. Twelve beds at eighteen-pence a bed—that's eighteen shillings; and say ten bob in various drinks and the stuff we brought with us, that's two pound twelve.

That publican didn't do so bad out of us in two hours.'

We wondered how much the driver got out of it, but thought it best not to ask him.

We didn't say much for the rest of the journey. There was the usual man who thought as much and knew all about it from the first, but he wasn't appreciated. We suppressed him. One or two wanted to go back and 'stoush' that landlord, and the driver stopped the coach cheerfully at their request; but they said they'd come across him again, and allowed themselves to be persuaded out of it. It made us feel bad to think how we had allowed ourselves to be delayed, and robbed, and had sneaked round on tiptoe, and how we had sat on the inoffensive pilgrim and his mate, and all on account of a sick wife who didn't exist.

The coach arrived at Dead Camel in an atmosphere of mutual suspicion and distrust, and we spread ourselves over the train and departed.

HENRY LAWSON

The Buck-jumper

From Joe Wilson's Mates *(Sydney, 1904)*.

Saturday afternoon.

There were about a dozen bush natives, from anywhere, most of them lanky and easygoing, hanging about the little slab-and-bark hotel on the edge of the scrub at Capertee Camp (a teamster's camp) when Cobb & Co.'s mail-coach and six came dashing down the sidling from round Crown Ridge, in all its glory, to the end of the 12-mile stage. Some dusty, wiry, ill-used hacks were hanging to the fence and to saplings about the place. The fresh coach-horses stood ready in a stockyard close to the shanty. As the coach climbed the nearer bank of the creek at the foot of the ridge, six of the bushmen detached themselves from veranda-posts, from their heels, from the clay floor of the veranda and the rough slab wall against which they'd been resting, and joined a group of four or five who stood round one. He stood with his back to the corner post of the stockyard, his feet well braced out in front of him, and contemplated the toes of his tight new 'lastic-side boots and whistled softly. He was a clean-limbed, handsome fellow, with riding-cords, leggings, and a blue sash; he was Graeco-Roman-nosed, blue-eyed, and his glossy, curly black hair bunched up in front of the brim of a new cabbage-tree hat, set well back on his head.

'Do it for a quid, Jack?' asked one.

'Damned if I will, Jim!' said the young man at the post. 'I'll do it for a fiver—not a blanky sprat less.'

Jim took off his hat and 'shoved' it round, and 'bobs' were

91

'chucked' into it. The result was about 30 shillings.

Jack glanced contemptuously into the crown of the hat.

'Not me!' he said, showing some emotion for the first time. 'D'yer think I'm going to risk me blanky neck for your blanky amusement for thirty blanky bob? I'll ride the blanky horse for a fiver, and I'll feel the blanky quids in my pocket before I get on.'

Meanwhile the coach had dashed up to the door of the shanty. There were about 20 passengers aboard—inside, on the box seat, on the tail-board, and hanging on to the roof—most of them Sydney men going up to the Mudgee races. They got down and went inside with the driver for a drink, while the stablemen changed horses. The bushmen raised their voices a little and argued.

One of the passengers was a big, stout, hearty man—a good-hearted, sporting man and a racehorse owner, according to his brands. He had a round red face and white cork hat. 'What's those chaps got on outside?' he asked the publican.

'Oh, it's a bet they've got on about riding a horse,' replied the publican. 'The flash-looking chap with the sash is Flash Jack, the horse-breaker; and they reckon they've got the champion outlaw in the district out there—that chestnut horse in the yard.'

The sporting man was interested at once, and went out and joined the bushmen.

'Well, chaps! what have you got on here?' he asked cheerily.

'Oh,' said Jim carelessly, 'it's only a bit of a bet about ridin' that blanky chestnut in the corner of the yard there.' He indicated an ungroomed chestnut horse, fenced off by a couple of long sapling poles in a corner of the stockyard. 'Flash Jack there—he reckons he's the champion horse-breaker round here—Flash Jack reckons he can take it out of that horse first try.'

'What's up with the horse?' inquired the big, red-faced man. 'It looks quiet enough. Why, I'd ride it myself.'

'Would yer?' said Jim, who had hair that stood straight up, and an innocent, inquiring expression. 'Looks quiet, does he? *You* ought to know more about horses than to go by the looks of 'em. He's quiet enough just now, when there's no one near him; but you should have been here an hour ago. That horse has killed two men and put another chap's shoulder out—besides breaking a cove's leg. It took six of us all the morning to run him in and get the saddle on him; and now Flash Jack wants to back out of it.'

'Euraliar!' remarked Flash Jack cheerfully. 'I said I'd ride that blanky horse out of the yard for a fiver. I ain't goin' to risk my blanky neck for nothing and only to amuse you blanks.'

'He said he'd ride the horse inside the yard for a quid,' said Jim.

'And get smashed against the rails!' said Flash Jack. 'I would be a fool. I'd rather take my chance outside in the scrub—and it's rough country round here.'

'Well, how much do you want?' asked the man in the mushroom hat.

'A fiver, I said,' replied Jack indifferently. 'And the blanky stuff in my pocket before I get on the blanky horse.'

'Are you frightened of us running away without paying you?' inquired one of the passengers who had gathered round.

'I'm frightened of the horse bolting with me without me being paid,' said Flash Jack. 'I know that horse; he's got a mouth like iron. I might be at the bottom of the cliff on Crown Ridge road in 20 minutes with my head caved in, and then what chance for the quids?'

'You wouldn't want 'em then,' suggested a passenger. 'Or, say!—we'd leave the fiver with the publican to bury you.'

Flash Jack ignored that passenger. He eyed his boots and softly whistled a tune.

'All right!' said the man in the cork hat, putting his hand in his pocket. 'I'll start with a quid; stump up, you chaps.'

The five pounds were got together.

'I'll lay a quid to half a quid he don't stick on ten minutes!' shouted Jim to his mates as soon as he saw that the event was to come off. The passengers also betted amongst themselves. Flash Jack, after putting the money in his breeches-pocket, let down the rails and let the horse into the middle of the yard.

'Quiet as an old cow!' snorted a passenger in disgust. 'I believe it's a sell!'

'Wait a bit,' said Jim to the passenger, 'wait a bit and you'll see.'

They waited and saw.

Flash Jack leisurely mounted the horse, rode slowly out of the yard, and trotted briskly round the corner of the shanty and into the scrub, which swallowed him more completely than the sea might have done.

Most of the other bushmen mounted their horses and followed Flash Jack to a clearing in the scrub, at a safe distance from the shanty; then they dismounted and hung on to saplings, or leaned against their horses, while they laughed.

At the hotel there was just time for another drink. The driver climbed to his seat and shouted, 'All aboard!' in his usual tone. The passengers climbed to their places, thinking hard. A mile or so along the road the man with the cork hat remarked, with much truth:

'Those blanky bushmen have got too much time to think.' The bushmen returned to the shanty as soon as the coach was out of sight, and proceeded to 'knock down' the fiver.

HENRY LAWSON

The Hypnotized Township

From The Rising of the Court and Other Sketches in Prose and
Verse *(Sydney, 1910)*.

———————

They said that Harry Chatswood, the mail contractor would do
anything for Cobb & Co., even to stretching fencing-wire across
the road in a likely place: but I don't believe that—Harry was too
good-hearted to risk injuring innocent passengers, and he had a
fellow feeling for drivers, being an old coach driver on rough outback tracks himself. But he did rig up fencing-wire for old Mac,
the carrier, one night, though not across the road. Harry, by the
way, was a city-born bushman, who had been everything for
some years. Anything from six-foot-six to six-foot-nine, 14 stone,
and a hard case. He is a very successful coach-builder now, for he
knows the wood, the roads, and the weak parts in a coach.

It was in the good seasons when competition was keen and
men's hearts were hard—not as it is in times of drought, when
there is no competition, and men's hearts are soft, and there is all
kindness and goodwill between them. He had had much
opposition in fighting Cobb & Co., and his coaches had won
through on the outer tracks. There was little malice in his
composition, but when old Mac, the teamster, turned his teams
over to his sons and started a light van for parcels and passengers
from Cunnamulla—that place which always sounds to me
suggestive of pumpkin pies—out in seeming opposition to Harry
Chatswood, Harry was annoyed.

Perhaps Mac only wished to end his days on the road with
parcels that were light and easy to handle (not like loads of

fencing wire) and passengers that were sociable; but he had been doing well with his teams, and, besides, Harry thought he was after the mail contract: so Harry was annoyed more than he was injured. Mac was mean with the money he had—not because of the money he had a chance of getting; and he mostly slept in his van, in all weathers, when away from home which was kept by his wife about half-way between the half-way house and the next 'township'.

One dark, gusty evening, Harry Chatswood's coach dragged, heavily though passengerless into Cunnamulla, and, as he turned into the yard of the local 'Royal', he saw Mac's tilted four-wheeler (which he called his 'van') drawn up opposite by the kerbing round the post office. Mac always chose a central position—with a vague idea of advertisement perhaps. But the nearness to the P.O. reminded Harry of the mail contracts, and he knew that Mac had taken up a passenger or two and some parcels in front of him (Harry) on the trip in. And something told Harry that Mac was asleep inside his van. It was a windy night, with signs of rain, and the curtains were drawn close.

Old Mac was there all right, and sleeping the sleep of a tired driver after a long drowsy day on a hard box seat, with little or no back railing to it. But there was a lecture on, or an exhibition of hypnotism or mesmerism—'a blanky spirit rappin' fake,' they called it, run by 'some blanker' in 'the hall'; and when old Mac had seen to his horses, he thought he might as well drop in for half an hour and see what was going on. Being a Mac, he was, of course, theological, scientific, and argumentative. He saw some things which woke him up, challenged the performer to hyp-notize him, was 'operated' on or 'fooled with' a bit, had a 'numb sorter light-headed feelin',' and was told by a voice from the back of the hall that his 'leg was being pulled, Mac,' and by another buzzin' far-away kind of 'ventrillick' voice that he would make a good subject, and that, if he only had the will power and knew how (which he would learn from a book the professor had to sell for five shillings) he would be able to drive his van without horses or anything, save the pole sticking straight out in front. These

weren't the professor's exact words——But, anyway, Mac came
to himself with a sudden jerk, left with a great Scottish snort of
disgust and the sound of heavy boots along the floor; and after a
resentful whisky at the Royal, where they laughed at his
scrooging bushy eyebrows, fierce black eyes and his deadly-in-
earnest denunciation of all humbugs and impostors, he returned
to the aforesaid van, let down the flaps, buttoned the daft and
'feekle' world out, and himself in, and then retired some more
and slept, as I have said, rolled in his blankets and overcoats on a
bed of cushions and chaff-bags.

Harry Chatswood got down from his empty coach, and was
helping the yard boy take out the horses, when his eye fell on the
remnant of a roll of fencing-wire standing by the stable wall in the
light of the lantern. Then an idea struck him unexpectedly, and his
mind became luminous. He unhooked the swingle-bar, swung it
up over his 'leader's' rump (he was driving only three horses that
trip), and hooked it on to the horns of the hames. Then he went
inside (there was another light there) and brought out a bridle
and an old pair of spurs that were hanging on the wall. He
buckled on the spurs at the chopping block, slipped the winkers
off the leader and the bridle on, and took up the fencing-wire,
and started out the gate with the horse. The boy gaped after him
once, and then hurried to put up the other two horses. He knew
Harry Chatswood, and was in a hurry to see what he would be up
to.

There was a good crowd in town for the show, or the races, or a
stock sale, or land ballot, or something; but most of them were
tired, or at tea—or in the pubs—and the corners were deserted.
Observe how fate makes time and things fit when she wants to do
a good turn—or play a practical joke. Harry Chatswood, for
instance, didn't know anything about the hypnotic business.

It was the corners of the main street or road and the principal
short cross street, and the van was opposite the pub stables in the
main street. Harry crossed the streets diagonally to the opposite
corner, in a line with the van. There he slipped the bar down over
the horse's rump, and fastened one end of the wire on to the ring

of it. Then he walked back to the van, carrying the wire and letting the coils go wide, and, as noiselessly as possible, made a loop in the loose end and slipped it over the hooks on the end of the pole. ('Unnecessary detail!' my contemporaries will moan, 'Overloaded with uninteresting details!' But that's because they haven't got the details—and it's the details that go.) Then Harry skipped back to his horse, jumped on, gathered up the bridle reins, and used his spurs. There was a swish and a clang, a scrunch and a clock-clock and rattle of wheels, and a surprised human sound; then a bump and a shout—for there was no underground drainage, and the gutters belonged to the Stone Age. There was a swift clocking and rattle, more shouts, another bump, and a yell. And so on down the longish main street. The stable-boy, who had left the horses in his excitement, burst into the bar, shouting, 'The Hypnertism's on, the Mesmerism's on! Ole Mac's van's runnin' away with him without no horses all right!' The crowd scuffled out into the street; there were some unfortunate horses hanging up of course at the panel by the pub trough, and the first to get to them jumped on and rode; the rest ran. The hall—where they were clearing the willing professor out in favour of a 'darnce'—and the other pubs decanted their contents, and chance souls skipped for the verandas of weather-board shanties out of which other souls popped to see the runaway. They saw a weird horseman, or rather, something like a camel (for Harry rode low, like Tod Sloan with his long back humped—for effect)—apparently fleeing for its life in a veil of dust, along the long white road, and some forty rods behind, an unaccountable tilted coach careered in its own separate cloud of dust. And from it came the shouts and yells. Men shouted and swore, women screamed for their children, and kids whimpered. Some of the men turned with an oath and stayed the panic with:

'It's only one of them flamin' motor-cars, you fools.'

It might have been, and the yells the warning howls of a motorist who had burst or lost his honk-konk and his head.

'It's runnin' away!' or 'The toff's mad or drunk!' shouted others. 'It'll break its crimson back over the bridge.'

'Let it!' was the verdict of some. 'It's all the crimson carnal things are good for.'

But the riders still rode and the footmen ran. There was a clatter of hoofs on the short white bridge looming ghostly ahead, and then, at a weird interval, the rattle and rumble of wheels, with no hoof-beats accompanying. The yells grew fainter. Harry's leader was a good horse, of the rather heavy coach-horse breed, with a little of the racing blood in her, but she was tired to start with, and only excitement and fright at the feel of the 'pull' of the twisting wire kept her up that speed; and now she was getting winded, so half a mile or so beyond the bridge Harry thought it had gone far enough, and he stopped and got down. The van ran on a bit, of course, and the loop of the wire slipped off the hooks of the pole. The wire recoiled itself roughly along the dust nearly to the heels of Harry's horse. Harry grabbed up as much of the wire as he could claw for, took the mare by the neck with the other hand, and vanished through the dense fringe of scrub off the road, till the wire caught and pulled him up; he stood still for a moment, in the black shadow on the edge of a little clearing, to listen. Then he fumbled with the wire until he got it untwisted, cast it off, and moved off silently with the mare across the soft rotten ground, and left her in a handy bush stockyard, to be brought back to the stables at a late hour that night—or rather an early hour next morning—by a jackeroo stable-boy who would have two half-crowns in his pocket and afterthought instructions to look out for that wire and hide it if possible.

Then Harry Chatswood got back quickly, by a roundabout way, and walked into the bar of the Royal, through the back entrance from the stables, and stared, and wanted to know where all the chaps had gone to, and what the noise was about, and whose trap had run away, and if anybody was hurt.

The growing crowd gathered round the van, silent and awe-struck, and some of them threw off their hats, and lost them, in their anxiety to show respect for the dead, or render assistance to the hurt, as men do, round a bad accident in the bush. They got the old man out, and two of them helped him back along the road, with great solicitude, while some walked round the van, and swore beneath their breaths, or stared at it with open mouths, or examined it curiously, with their eyes only, and in breathless silence. They muttered, and agreed, in the pale moonlight now showing, that the sounds of the horses' hoofs had only been 'spirit-rappin' sounds;' and, after some more muttering, two of the stoutest, with subdued oaths, laid hold of the pole and drew the van to the side of the road, where it would be out of the way of chance night traffic. But they stretched and rubbed their arms afterwards, and then, and on the way back, they swore to admiring acquaintances that they felt the 'blanky 'lectricity' runnin' all up their arms and 'elbers' while they were holding the pole, which, doubtless, they did—in imagination.

They got old Mac back to the Royal, with sundry hasty whiskies on the way. He was badly shaken, both physically, mentally, and in his convictions, and, when he'd pulled himself together, he had little to add to what they already knew. But he confessed that, when he got under his possum rug in the van, he couldn't help thinking of the professor and his creepy (it was 'creepy,' or 'uncanny,' or 'awful,' or 'rum' with 'em now)—his blanky creepy hypnotism; and he (old Mac) had just laid on his back comfortable, and stretched his legs out straight, and his arms down straight by his sides, and drew long, slow breaths, and tried to fix his mind on nothing—as the professor had told him when he was 'operatin' on him' in the hall. Then he began to feel a strange sort of numbness coming over him, and his limbs went heavy as lead, and he seemed to be gettin' light-headed. Then, all on a sudden, his arms seemed to begin to lift, and just when he was goin' to pull 'em down the van started as they had heard and seen it. After a while he got on to his knees and managed to wrench a corner of the front curtain clear of the button and get his head out. And there was the van going helter-skelter, and feeling like Tam o'Shanter's mare (the old man said), and he on her bare-backed. And there was no horses, but a cloud of dust—or a spook—on ahead, and the bare pole steering straight for it, just as the professor had said it would be. The old man thought he was going to be taken clear across the Never-Never country and left to roast on a sandhill, hundreds of miles from anywhere, for his sins, and he said he was trying to think of a prayer or two all the time he was yelling. They handed him more whisky from the publican's own bottle. Hushed and cautious inquiries for the Professor (with a big P now) elicited the hushed and cautious fact that he had gone to bed. But old Mac caught the awesome name and glared round, so they hurriedly filled out another for him, from the boss's bottle. Then there was a slight commotion. The housemaid hurried scaredly in to the bar behind and whispered to the boss. She had been startled nearly out of her wits by the Professor suddenly appearing at his bedroom door and calling upon her to have a stiff nobbler of whisky hot sent up to his room. The jackeroo yard-boy, aforesaid, volunteered to take it up, and while he was gone there were hints of hysterics from the kitchen, and the boss whispered in his turn to the crowd over the bar. The jackeroo just handed the tray and glass in through the partly opened door, had a glimpse of pyjamas, and, after what seemed an interminable wait, he came tiptoeing into the bar amongst its awe-struck haunters with an air of great mystery, and no news whatever.

They fixed old Mac on a shake-down in the Commercial Room, where he'd have light and some overflow guests on the sofas for company. With a last whisky in the bar, and a stiff whisky by his side on the floor, he was understood to chuckle to the effect that he knew he was all right when he'd won 'the keystone o' the brig.' Though how a wooden bridge with a level plank floor could have a keystone I don't know—and they were too much impressed by the event of the evening to inquire. And so, with a few cases of hysterics to occupy the attention of the younger women, some whimpering of frightened children and comforting or chastened nagging by mothers, some unwonted prayers muttered secretly and forgettingly, and a good deal of subdued blasphemy, Cunnamulla sank to its troubled slumbers—some of the sleepers in the commercial and billiard-rooms and parlours at the Royal, to start up in a cold sweat, out of their beery and hypnotic nightmares, to find Harry Chatswood making elaborate and fearsome passes over them with his long, gaunt arms and hands, and a flaming red table-cloth tied round his neck.

To be done with old Mac, for the present. He made one or two more trips, but always by daylight, taking care to pick up a swagman or a tramp when he had no passenger; but his 'conveections' had had too much of a shaking, so he sold his turn-out (privately and at a distance, for it was beginning to be called 'the haunted van') and returned to his teams—always keeping one of the lads with him for company. He reckoned it would take the devil's own hypnotism to move a load of fencing-wire, or pull a wool-team of bullocks out of a bog; and before he invoked the ungodly power, which he let them believe he could—he'd stick there and starve till he and his bullocks died a 'natural' death. (He was a bit Irish—as all Scots are—back on one side.)

But the strangest is to come. The Professor, next morning, proved uncomfortably unsociable, and though he could have done a roaring business that night—and for a week of nights after, for that matter—and though he was approached several times, he, for some mysterious reason known only to himself, flatly refused to give one more performance, and said he was leaving the town that day. He couldn't get a vehicle of any kind, for fear, love, or money, until Harry Chatswood, who took a day off, volunteered, for a stiff consideration, to borrow a buggy and drive him (the Professor) to the next town towards the then railway terminus, in which town the Professor's fame was not so awesome, and where he might get a lift to the railway. Harry ventured to remark to the Professor once or twice during the drive that 'there was a rum business with old Mac's van last night,' but he could get nothing out of him, so gave it best, and finished the journey in contemplative silence.

Now, the fact was that the Professor had been the most surprised and startled man in Cunnamulla that night; and he brooded over the thing till he came to the conclusion that hypnotism was a dangerous power to meddle with unless a man was physically and financially strong and carefree—which he wasn't. So he threw it up.

He learnt the truth, some years later, from a brother of Harry Chatswood, in a Home or Retreat for Geniuses, where 'friends were paying,' and his recovery was so sudden that it surprised and disappointed the doctor and his friend, the manager of the home. As it was, the Professor had some difficulty in getting out of it.

HENRY LAWSON

The Exciseman

From The Rising of the Court and Other Sketches in Prose and
Verse *(Sydney, 1910)*.

Harry Chatswood, mail contractor (and several other things),
was driving out from, say, Georgeville to Croydon, with mails,
parcels, and only one passenger—a commercial traveller, who
had shown himself unsociable, and close in several other ways.
Nearly half-way to a place that was half-way between the half-
way house and the town, Harry overhauled 'Old Jack,' a local
character (there are many well-known characters named 'Old
Jack'), and gave him a lift as a matter of course.

'Hello! Is that you, Jack?' in the gathering dusk.

'Yes, Harry.'

'Then jump up here.'

Harry was good-natured and would give anybody a lift if he
could.

Old Jack climbed up on the box seat, between Harry and the
traveller, who grew rather more stand- (or rather *sit-*) offish,
wrapped himself closer in his overcoat, and buttoned his cloak of
silence and general disgust to the chin button. Old Jack got his
pipe to work and grunted, and chatted, and exchanged bush
compliments with Harry comfortably. And so on to where they
saw the light of a fire outside a hut ahead.

'Let me down here, Harry,' said Old Jack uneasily. 'I owe
Mother Mac fourteen shillings for drinks, and I haven't got it on
me, and I've been on the spree back yonder, and she'll know it,
an' I don't want to face her. I'll cut across through the paddock

and you can pick me up on the other side.'

Harry thought a moment.

'Sit still, Jack,' he said. 'I'll fix that all right.' He twisted and went down into his trouser-pocket, the reins in one hand, and brought up a handful of silver. He held his hand down to the coach lamp, separated some of the silver from the rest by a sort of sleight of hand—or rather sleight of fingers—and handed the 14 shillings over to Old Jack.

'Here y'are, Jack. Pay me some other time.'

'Thanks, Harry!' grunted Old Jack, as he twisted for *his* pocket.

It was a cold night, the hint of a possible shanty thawed the traveller a bit, and he relaxed with a couple of grunts about the weather and the road, which were received in a brotherly spirit. Harry's horses stopped of their own accord in front of the house, an old bark-and-slab whitewashed humpy of the eary settlers' farm-house type, with a plank door in the middle, one bleary-lighted window on one side, and one forbiddingly blind one, as if death were there, on the other. It might have been. The door opened, letting out a flood of lamp-light and firelight which blindly showed the sides of the coach and the near pole horse and threw the coach lamps nd the rest into the outer darkness of the opposing bush.

'Is that you, Harry?' called a voice and tone like Mrs Warren's of the Profession.

'It's me.'

A stoutly, aggressive woman appeared. She was rather florid, and looked, moved and spoke as if she had been something in the city in other years, and had been dumped down in the bush to make money in mysterious ways; had married, mated—or got herself to be supposed to be married—for convenience, and continued to make money by mysterious means. Anyway, she was 'Mother Mac' to the bush, but, in the bank in the 'town', and in the stores where she dealt, she was *Mrs* Mac, and there was always a promptly propped chair for her. She was, indeed, the missus of no other than old Mac, the teamster of hypnotic fame, and late opposition to Harry Chatswood. Hence, perhaps, part of Harry's hesitation to pull up, farther back, and his generosity to Old Jack.

Mrs or Mother Mac sold refreshments from a rough bush dinner at eighteenpence a head to passengers, to a fly-blown bottle of ginger-ale or lemonade, hot in hot weather from a sunny fly-specked window. In between there was cold corned beef, bread and butter, and tea, and (best of all if they only knew it) a good bush billy of coffee on the coals before the fire on cold wet nights. And outside of it all, there was cold tea, which, when confidence was established, or they knew one of the party, she served hushedly in cups without saucers; for which she sometimes apologized, and which she took into her murderous bedroom to fill, and replenish, in its darkest and most felonious corner from homicidal-looking pots, by candle-light. You'd think you were in a cheap place, where you shouldn't be, in the city.

Harry and his passengers got down and stretched their legs, and while Old Jack was guardedly answering a hurriedly whispered inquiry of the traveller, Harry took the opportunity to nudge Mrs Mac, and whisper in her ear:

'Look out, Mrs Mac!—Exciseman!'

'The devil he is!' whispered she.

'Ye-e-es!' whispered Harry.

'All right, Harry!' she whispered. 'Never a word! I'll take care of him, bless his soul.'

After a warm at the wide wood fire, a gulp of coffee and a bite or two at the bread and meat, the traveller, now thoroughly thawed, stretched himself and said:

'Ah, well, Mrs Mac, haven't you got anything else to offer us?'

'And what more would you be wanting?' she snapped. 'Isn't the bread and meat good enough for you?'

'But—but—you know——' he suggested lamely.

'Know?—I know!—What do *I* know?' A pause, then, with startling suddenness, 'Phwat d'y' mean?'

'No offence, Mrs Mac—no offence; but haven't you got something in the way of—of a drink to offer us?'

'Dhrink! Isn't the coffee good enough for ye? I paid two and six a pound for ut, and the milk new from the cow this very evenin'— an' th' water rain-water.'

'But—but—you know what I mean, Mrs Mac.'

'An' I *don't* know what ye mean. *Phwat do ye mean?* I've asked ye that before. What are ye dhrivin' at, man—out with it!'

'Well, I mean a little drop of the right stuff,' he said, nettled. Then he added: 'No offence—no harm done.'

'O-o-oh!' she said, illumination bursting in upon her brain. 'It's the dirty drink ye're afther, is it? Well, I'll tell ye, first for last, that we doan't keep a little drop of the right stuff nor a little drop of the wrong stuff in this house. It's a honest house, an' me husband's a honest harrd-worrkin' carrier, as he'd soon let ye know if he was at home this cold night, poor man. No dirrty drink comes into this house, nor goes out of it, I'd have ye know.'

'Now, now, Mrs Mac, between friends, I meant no offence; but it's a cold night, and I thought you might keep a bottle for medicine—or in case of accident—or snake-bite, you know— they mostly do in the bush.'

'Medicine! And phwat should we want with medicine? This isn't a five-guinea private hospital. We're clean, healthy people, I'd have ye know. There's a bottle of painkiller, if that's what ye want, and a packet of salts left—maybe they'd do ye some good. An' a bottle of eye-water, an' something to put in your ear for th' earache—maybe ye'll want 'em both before ye go much farther.'

'But, Mrs Mac——'

'No, no more of it!' she said. 'I tell ye that if it's a nip ye're after, ye'll have to go on fourteen miles to the pub in the town. Ye're coffee's gittin' cowld, an' it's eighteenpence each to passengers I charge on a night like this; Harry Chatswood's the driver an' welcome, an' Ould Jack's an ould friend.' And she flounced round to clatter her feelings amongst the crockery on the dresser—just as men make a great show of filling and lighting their pipes in the middle of a barney. The table, by the way, was set on a brown holland cloth, with the brightest of tin plates for cold meals, and the brigtest of tin pint-pots for the coffee (the crockery was in reserve for hot meals and special local occasions) and at one side of the wide fire-place hung an old-fashioned fountain, while in the other stood a camp-oven; and billies and a black kerosene-tin hung evermore over the fire from sooty chains. These, and a big bucket-handled frying-pan and a few rusty convict-time arms on the slab walls, were mostly to amuse jackeroos and jackerooesses, and let them think they were getting into the Australian-dontcherknow at last.

Harry Chatswood took the opportunity (he had a habit of taking opportunities of this sort) to whisper to Old Jack:

'Pay her the fourteen bob, Jack, and have done with it. She's got the needle to-night all right, and damfiknow what for. But the sight of your fourten bob might bring her round.' And Old Jack—as was his way—blundered obediently and promptly right into the hole that was shown him.

'Well, Mrs Mac,' he said, getting up from the table and slipping his hand into his pocket. 'I don't know what's come over yer to-night, but, anyway——' Here he put the money down on the table. 'There's the money I owe yer for—for——'

'For what?' she demanded, turning on him with surprising swiftness for such a stout woman.

'The—the fourteen bob I owed for them drinks when Bill Hogan and me——'

'You don't owe me no fourteen bob for dhrinks, you dirty blaggard! Are ye mad? You got no drink off me. Phwat d'ye mean?'

'Beg—beg pardin, Mrs Mac,' stammered Old Jack, very much taken aback; 'but the—yer know—the fourteen bob, anyway, I owed you when—that night when me an' Bill Hogan an' yer sister-in-law, Mary Don——'

'What? Well, I—Git out of me house, ye low blaggard! I'm a honest, respictable married woman, and so is me sister-in-law, Mary Donelly; and to think!—Git out of me door!' and she caught up the billy of coffee. 'Git outside me door, or I'll let ye have it in ye'r ugly face, ye low woolscourer—an' it's nearly bilin'.'

Old Jack stumbled dazedly out, and blind instinct got him on to the coach as the safest place. Harry Chatswood had stood with his long, gaunt figure hung by an elbow to the high mantel-shelf, all the time, taking alternate gulps from his pint of coffee and puffs from his pipe, and very calmly and restfully regarding the scene.

'An' now,' she said, 'if the *gentleman*'s done, I'd thank him to pay—it's eighteenpence—an' git his overcoat on. I've had enough dirty insults this night to last me a lifetime. To think of it—the blaggard!' she said to the table, 'an' me a woman alone in a place like this on a night like this!'

The traveller calmly put down a two-shilling piece, as if the whole affair was the most ordinary thing in the world (for he was used to many bush things) and comfortably got into his overcoat.

'Well, Mrs Mac, I never thought Old Jack was mad before,' said Harry Chatswood. 'And I hinted to him,' he added in a whisper. 'Anyway' (out loudly): 'you'll lend me a light, Mrs Mac, to have a look at that there swingle-bar of mine?'

'With pleasure, Harry,' she said, 'for you're a white man, anyway. I'll bring ye a light. An' all the lights in heaven if I could, an'—an' in the other place if they'd help ye.'

When he'd looked to the swingle-bar, and had mounted to his place and untwisted the reins from a side-bar, she cried:

'An' as for them two, Harry, shpill them in the first creek you come to, an' God be good to you! It's all they're fit for, the low blaggards, to insult an honest woman alone in the bush in a place like this.'

'All right, Mrs Mac,' said Harry, cheerfully. 'Good night, Mrs Mac.'

'Good night, Harry, an' God go with ye, for the creeks are risen after last night's storm.' And Harry drove on and left her to think over it.

She thought over it in a way that would have been unexpected to Harry, and would have made him uneasy, for he was really good-natured. She sat down on a stool by the fire, and presently, after thinking over it a bit, two big, lonely tears rolled down the lonely woman's fair, fat, blonde cheeks in the firelight.

'An' to think of Old Jack,' she said. 'The very last man in the world I'd dreamed of turning on me. But—but I always thought Old Jack was goin' a bit ratty, an' maybe I was a bit hard on him. God forgive us all!'

Had Harry Chatswood seen her then he would have been sorry he did it. Swagmen and broken-hearted new chums had met worse women than Mother Mac.

But she pulled herself together, got up and bustled round. She put on more wood, swept the hearth, put a parcel of fresh steak and sausages—brought by the coach—on to a clean plate on the table, and got some potatoes into a dish; for Chatswood had told her that her first and longest and favourite stepson was not far behind him with the bullock team. Before she had finished the potatoes she heard the clock-clock of heavy wheels and the crack of the bullock whip coming along the dark bush track.

But the very next morning a man riding back from Croydon called, and stuck his head under the veranda eaves with a bush greeting, and she told him all about it.

He straightened up, and tickled the back of his head with his little finger, and gaped at her for a minute.

'Why,' he said, 'that wasn't no excise officer. I know him well—I was drinking with him at the Royal last night afore we went to bed, an' had a nip with him this morning afore we started. Why! that's Bobby Howell, Burns and Bridges's traveller, an' a good sort when he wakes up, an' willing with the money when he does good biz, especially when there's a chanst of a drink on a long road on a dark night.'

'That Harry Chastwood again! The infernal villain,' she cried, with a jerk of her arm. 'But I'll be even with him, the dirrty blaggard. An' to think—I always knew Old Jack was a white man an'—to think! There's fourteen shillin's gone that Old Jack would have paid me, an' the traveller was good for three shillin's f'r the nips, an'—but Old Jack will pay me next time, and I'll be even with Harry Chatswood, the dirrty mail carter. I'll take it out of him in parcels—I'll be even with him.'

She never saw Old Jack again with fourteen shillings, but she got even with Harry Chatswood, and——But I'll tell you about that some other time. Time for a last smoke before we turn in.

W. E. MEAD

The Fate of a Chinese Passenger

Quoted from The Lights of Cobb and Co: The Story of the Frontier Coaches, *by K. A. Austin (Seal Books, Adelaide, 1972). W. E. Mead's manuscript,* Reminiscences, *is held in the Cobb & Co. Transport Museum, Toowoomba, Queensland.*

In his reminiscences, former Cobb & Co. driver W. E. Mead tells of an amusing incident for which a driver was held responsible and censured, although it was not really his fault. It concerns Cobb & Co.'s driver on the Charleville-Augathella line in western Queensland, Bob Wright, who left Charleville one Saturday afternoon with a fourteen-passenger coach on his usual run:

'Bob had a team of eight horses full of life and go, and, as the Post Office was his last call, Bob had a look round to see that everything was alright. His passengers were all aboard, and amongst them was a Chinaman who was sitting right up on top of the coach, the only place where he could get a seat. There was also quite a heap of goods up there, and he was sitting on top of it. About one hundred yards from the Post Office was the bridge over the first channel of the Warrego River, and there was a limb from a coolibah tree growing across the bridge like an arm held straight out. Well, when Bob gave the word to go, the horses jumped out like a shot downhill to the bridge, and the Chinaman saw this limb coming towards him and he got scared, thinking it was going to scrape him off. (He would have been quite safe.) He put out both arms and grabbed the limb, and the coach went on without him. And when Bob got to the Pine Grove mail change

10 miles out, he walked around his coach, and looked up, and then said to a passenger inside the coach:

'"I thought I had a Chinaman up there when I left."

'The passenger said, "So there was."

'"Well," Bob said, "he's not there now."

And that was that. The police in Charleville had to get a ladder to get the Chinaman down, and Bob had a lot of explaining to do when he came back on Monday.'

WARREN DENNING

Razorback Road

From The Road to Canberra: The Story of a Highway *(Sydney, 1947). The 'Razorback' referred to is Razorback Mountain, New South Wales.*

———————

Some of the terrors of travel on Razorback were described in an article published in the *Sydney Morning Herald* in 1937, giving a first-hand picture of an episode (evidently written many years before and published from an old manuscript) which occurred in the days of Cobb & Co. The style of writing would have done credit to a police roundsman on a yellow journal:

'The evening was very stormy as the great southern mail coach wound its way down the side of the Razorback. The thunder rolled and the lightning flashed from every point of the compass. On the one hand were the deep, black unfathomable ravines where the foot of man has never trod, while on the other hand rose the vast mountainside, terrific in its grandeur . . . Suddenly there came a terrific blinding flash, a loud crash, and one of the kings of the forest fell from its height above, and lay stretched across our path. It was the work of an instant. The terrified horses made one astounding leap, and together with the coach were launched into the abyss below. When the horses made their fearful leap I was jerked out of my seat on the box into the body of the coach by the sudden movement. I felt the vehicle rolling and crashing down the mountainside, now striking the roots of a decayed or fallen tree, now falling from some terrace, until I became unconscious from the repeated blows I received.'

The upshot of it was the driver and horses were killed; the writer lived to tell his highly-coloured tale.

BILL WANNAN

Joe Hirschberg of Cobb & Co.

From Australasian Post *(Melbourne, 16 June, 1960)*.

———————

In the early years of the present century before the railway line was extended from Almaden, in North Queensland, out west to Forsayth, a Cobb & Co. coach used to cover that rough stretch of country across the Newcastle Range.

Grooms were posted about every 12 miles to supply fresh horses for the next stage, so the going must have been pretty tough.

The Cobb service was bought out by Love and Company round about 1907, and it was during this period that a correspondent, Mr P. Meggitt of Red Hill, Qld, used to ride occasionally on the coaches. He particularly remembered one of the drivers, a big Danish bloke named Joe Hirschberg:

'When riding on the box seat next to the big Dane, I'd be allowed to hold the reins while Joe lit a smoke. The weight of seven horses' heads, travelling at a fair pace, was as much as I could handle even for so short a time.

'I forget the name of the Governor of Queensland in those years, but anyway he was taking a trip to the Far North by special coach on one occasion and Joe Hirschberg was his driver. There was also a buckboard travelling with the convoy; it was used to carry the luggage and was being driven, if I remember aright, by the then State Treasurer, a man who was exceptionally skilled at handling horses.

'At one change there was a bit of trouble with the horses and in a haughty tone the Treasurer said, "Hirschberg, have these animals been in harness before?"

'Joe, ever the individualist, and not a man to be disconcerted by the high and mighty, replied gruffly, "Course they have. D'you think if they hadn't I'd let you bloody well drive 'em!"'

' "Well," said the Treasurer, "if you give me something better at the next changing post I'll cool down and not report you."'

'Said Joe indifferently, "Never mind. *You keep hot and report!*"'

'I've no idea where Joe Hirschberg is now [1960],' Mr Meggitt's letter concludes, 'but he was certainly a grand chap and always looked after the interests of his passengers.'

GUY E. MORTON EDEN

The Braidwood Coach

From Bush Ballads and Other Verses *(London, 1907)*.

Now, all aboard, my sonnies, for the time is slipping past,
We've got to make ten miles before the dawn,
Our team's a spankin' good' un, but they've never gone so fast
As they must to make the pace this blessed morn!

Just let that buckle out a hole! that's right—now mind your eye,
Or Thunderclap will catch you on the shin!
Are all the mailbags snug? Right-oh! whoa, Dingo! Narrabri!
Now, gentlemen, if *you* please—tumble in!
    Then whoa, steady, whoa! Now, let the beauties go—
    They know what they've to do before the dawnin';
And the journey ain't all clover, for the creek is runnin' over,
And we're bound to reach Moruya in the mornin'.

Just pass this rug across your knees and hitch it on the rail,
You'll find the air, sir, pretty cold and chill;
We can't pull up and light a fire when carryin' the mail,
We've got to freeze and bear it sittin' still!
Yes, dark it is, and some might find it difficult to steer,
For where the corners come it's hard to tell,
But I've been drivin' here, sir, somewhere close on twenty year
And I'd follow this old bush track by the smell!
    Then whoa, steady, whoa! Just hear the beauties go,
    All danger or fatigue they're simply scornin',

And no matter what the weather—you can bet they'll pull
    together
And will land us in Moruya in the mornin'!

I met a boundary rider just afore we started out
Who told me that the creek is rising fast;
I've crossed it flooded over, must be twenty times about,
And always prayed each time would be the last!
The water rushes onward in a swirl of crested foam,
Full three foot deep when taken at the flood,
And landed in the middle—well—you somehow sigh for home
When buried to the axles deep in mud!
    Then whoa, steady, whoa! Just see the beauties go,
    They know that soon will come the golden dawnin',
But if pluck and nerve can do it, you can bet they'll see us
    through it
And will land us in Moruya in the mornin'!

Just look how old Red Rover, like a young unbroken colt,
Lays down to it at whisper of his name,
I tell you he's a good 'un—my Colonial, what a jolt!
Oh no, sir, don't be sorry that you came!
Hurrah! the dawn is breakin'! now the gum-trees you can see
Like spectres tall and grim on either hand.
Let's reach the creek at daylight, and I then won't care a d——
It's a terror in the dark you understand!
    Then whoa, steady, whoa! Just see the darlin's go,
    Old Dingo cocks his ears by way of warnin'!
Keep up your heart, my beauty, just for me and home and duty,
And we're bound to reach Moruya in the mornin'!

We're getting very near, sir, and the creek will heave in sight
When once we round the tea-tree now in view;
Just close your eyes a moment, sir, and pray with all your might
That I may get the mailbags safely through—
Lay down to it, me darlin's, for the sake of auld lang syne,

Don't fail me, beauties, now we've come so far,
Another fifty yards we'll have the tea-tree well in line;
Hang on, sir, round the corner—here we are!
  Then whoa, steady, whoa! Lord! how the waters flow,
   See how the white foam glistens in the dawnin',
Lord knows if we shall do it—but I'm bound to rush 'em
  through it
If we want to reach Moruya in the mornin'!

Are all you chaps inside awake? That's right, well mind your eye,
The creek must be quite three foot deep or more,
You'd best get on the seat if you'd prefer to come through dry,
The water's bound to cover all the floor—
It's neck or nothin' now, sir, for we can't afford to shrink,
The creek gets only bigger with delay,
Hold on, sir, like blue blazes! for we're comin' to the brink!
Now, Thunderclap and Dingo, show the way!
  Now go, beauties, go! See how they breast the flow
   And face the stream, all danger simply scornin';
Now, Narrabri! Red Rover! one more pull! Hurrah, we're over!
And thank God we'll reach Moruya in the mornin'!

'Now, then, Out you Get!'

From Life in the Australian Backblocks *(Melbourne, 1911)*.

Travellers who have been used to macadamised highways can't
readily accommodate themselves to the altered conditions
pertaining to the back country, where there are only little
patches of made roads, mostly beside the wayside pubs (where
the publicans don't want them), no bridges or culverts cross the
creeks, and the distance from house to house ranges from twenty
to fifty miles. The bush track winds like a serpent across the hills
and through the forests of mulga and gidgee, whilst over the soft
sand-beds the tracks are as manifold as the beds and billabongs of
an inland river, showing the many deviations made by drivers in
their desire to save their horses. The latter, fed mostly on scrub
and saltbush, are not always in the pink of condition, and the
long stages, ranging up to 36 miles, together with the immense
loads that are piled on the vehicles, don't assist the animals in
keeping their ribs hidden. A team is often made up of anything
handy—little and big, light and heavy, and it may represent
several owners. Settlers give the coach-driver their half-broken
colts to quieten; and when a man has a horse that kicks, bolts,
jibs, or displays other peculiarities that the owner objects to, the
remedy is a few trips in the body of the coach team. These casual
horses may also be one-eyed, near-sighted, or purblind, but the
driver is glad to have their help.

I often heard admiring comments from visitors on the horses
that came spanking into Broken Hill with heavy loads from north
and west. These were the show horses. They had good roads to

travel on, and had to cut out their stage in record time to make up for the deficiencies of relays farther out. Mail-time is reckoned by minutes in Broken Hill; but when you inquire at the little places towards the border as to what time last week's 'Bulletin' will arrive, the answer is: 'Some time this afternoon, or to-night, or to-morrow.' A few points of rain on the track, though it would not stop a Chinaman from watering his cabbages, may delay the mail 48 hours. Tibooburra is advised by wire what time the coach leaves Milparinka, 24 miles distant; yet the people cannot tell within two or three hours, in average weather, when it will arrive. 'Heavy load' means late arrival, 'light load' early.

Sitting behind knocked-up horses on a hot summer's day, with dust and flies for an accompaniment to the creaking of wheels and the rocking of a crawling coach, is an experience that the far-back traveller can look forward to without fear of disappointment. Sometimes, to avoid being stuck up, he has to walk over the bad places, and even dig away the sand and mud with a shovel and spoke the wheels. One western line traversed many heavy sandbeds. On coming to one of these the driver would call out, 'Now, then, out you get!' and women and all would have to step out and tramp until the horses were able to trot again. But the westerners are used to that sort of thing, and willingly walk and graft a lot of the way over which they've paid anything from sixpence to ninepence a mile for the luxury of riding.

The commercial traveller is an objectionable passenger to a coach-driver at such times. His tin trunks are numerous, and their weight would knock up a mule team. He is generally a heavy person, too, and he doesn't like stepping down into a quagmire. When it is necessary to open a gate or to hook a trace-chain that has come undone he takes a tighter grip of his cigar and holds out his hand for the reins. But the commercial is a good fellow. He has always a fund of anecdote, and is usually provided with something in a bottle to refresh the driver after a trying experience. He pays liberally for his ride, and he rides all the way.

On the 200 mile journey between Tibooburra and Broken Hill I and others, after sitting cramped up, numbed and shivering, for hours on a winter's night, have got out and walked five or six miles to the mail change for a cup of tea, and have then enjoyed an hour or more's sleep before the coach turned up. By this I do not wish to infer that the general run of Out-back coaches are slow affairs; but over portions of the rough tracks it isn't possible for them to travel at full walk, much less at full trot. Though the casual passenger grumbles at having to get along by his own volition, the weary whip, tied to his worn-out team, envies him his freedom, and wishes that he could walk away likewise. The exigencies of his calling require him to be on the box for 50 hours at a stretch, with only a day or two and at one end only a night's rest between trips. Winter and summer, sunshine and rain, he works all day and all night, and all next day and right on through the night again, without a spell, stopping only at the changes for fresh horses and refreshments—and refreshments on this route vary from eight to eighteen hours apart.

Where there is a long interval between houses, the 'change' may be simply a sapling yard and a bough shed. The groom is mostly a single man, living in a tent. His only work is to look after a few horses which run in the bush, groom them, and help the driver with the changing on mail days. The coach may pass only once or twice a week, up and down, and between whiles he has a pretty lonely time of it, seeing nobody but an odd swagman. Where a selector's hut is handy to the road the selector acts as groom, and his wife earns an honest penny by providing refreshments for driver and passengers.

At one place we walked nearly a mile off the road to an old roughly-built hut, where the groom's wife supplied a substantial dinner for two shillings a head. The dining-room was a bough-covered skillion at the back, and you sat on long forms before a narrow table made of packing-cases that called up recollections of shearers' huts. There was no tablecloth, but we didn't mind little things like that, nor did we complain when the baby under the table amused itself by counting our legs and undoing our bootlaces. Everything was spotlessly clean, the women were homely and chatty, and though mine host carved in a short-sleeved flannel, open at the neck and bearing signs of recent hard graft, we felt very grateful as we climbed on board again.

Besides these stopping-places there are dozens of bush post-offices along the road. These are simply candle boxes, lolly tins, or kerosene tins, nailed to trees and gate-posts. Hollow trees are also used, a small piece being cut out of the trunk, and a tin awning nailed above it. Such receptacles are usually convenient enough for the driver to draw up alongside and drop the mail in, and take out anything that has been left for him. They occur in places where no sign of life is visible, in the heart of the scrub, on the edge of a plain, and on thickly-timbered hills. At other places a horseman, or a girl, or a black boy will be waiting, sometimes with parcels which may be anything from a cabbage to a box of eggs. At night-time the tired passenger, after sitting and rocking through hours of monotony, occasionally brightens up at the sight of a light ahead, and inquires the name of the place. The driver tells him the name of the squattage, or whatever may be adjacent. When they pull up the passenger is disappointed to find only a man standing by the roadside with a lantern, having ridden or walked down to ascertain the whereabouts of a certain bullock team and how it was getting on, while the place the driver had named is two miles or more off the road. Swagmen's fires, too, blaze out here and there, and sometimes the men have a message for the coachman, a letter to be posted, or they want to know something about the track, where water is to be found, the distance of places, when shearing starts at Boulka Lake, and if Bancannia has cut out yet. Maybe they only want a pipe of tobacco, which, in the swagman's opinion, is sufficient cause to hold up the Royal Mail.

There are receiving offices here and there—at a wayside store, hotel, or mining camp. On mail days people gather from all directions at these places, the arrival of the coach being the most important event of their lives. The orders and messages a driver receives from them are many and various. One man wants a pound of tobacco from the store, another wants a pair of boots or a pair of pants, a third hands him a bill with the amount and asks him to be good enough to get a receipt, and a fourth wants his dog registered. Mrs Brown passes up a pair of ducks, and would be obliged if he would give them to Mrs Smith, with her compliments, as he passes. Mrs Publichouse wants him, like a good fellow, to get her a cook or a housemaid in town. Another lady has been making jam, and desires several jars of it distributed among her friends along the track. Also McPherson wishes him to ask Anderson for the loan of his bay colt, and to bring it up alongside his team when he is coming back. These are a few of the innumerable favours which every coach-driver on the Outback roads is expected to do for nothing. If he forgets one of them, though it might be only a question concerning the health of Mrs Jones's baby, he will be told with sarcasm that 'he's got a head and so has a pin.'

We had a new experience at Packsaddle Bore, where the road crosses a wide, sandy creek. There had been rain in the neighbourhood, so the roads were heavy and creeks running. The up-coach was met here—bogged in mid-stream. The driver and a passenger were wading knee-deep in water, one at the horses' heads and one spoking, while a Chinaman, bound for a border squattage, handled the ribbons and shouted instructions from the box. 'Pullee gley orsee round more better!' he cried. 'Hit um the black one; my wor', lazy brute! Gee up, 'orsee! Gortam, whaffor?' We halted on the bank, and our leaders were transferred to the bogged team. Our amiable whip also stepped bare-legged into the water, and with their combined efforts the Royal Mail was rescued from the bog.

Now came our turn. Paddy, the driver, rushed them in so as to take the stiff part at a run. Alas! the pole-hook pulled out, and the leaders dashed away with the reins, leaving us stranded in the middle of the creek. Luckily the damage was easily repaired, and, there being plenty of horses, we got out of our difficulties after about an hour's delay.

The coach-driver bears a great deal more responsibility than he is given credit for. Think of the many steep and nasty gullies crossed in the dead of night; the deep gutters, begotten of old-time wheel-tracks, that run parallel with the road on the down grades, where the least swerve might mean a capsize; the twistings through scrub, where the track swings sharply round a stump or tree, or round the foot of a rugged ridge with the steep bank of a creek in juxtaposition, and you get some idea of what you owe to his steady hand, his keen eye, and his memory of the road, as he bowls you on through the long night. Half your time you can see nothing but a black bank before you, for through the sandbeds, over the stony plains and the powdery, grassless flats the road is invisible. Yet the horses swing on with an unfaltering stride that instils within you a sense of security. People whose avocations take them over many roads know how to appreciate a good whip ; they know what depends on the hand that holds the reins.

On very dark nights, when the skies are clouded, it occasionally happens that the road is missed. On a barren plain below Wonnaminta, where the track was hard to discern when starlit, we got astray one night, and were two hours searching with coach-lamps and matches for the track. Then there is always the dreaded north-west dust-storm to be reckoned with. Driving through one of these is worse than any night, for at times nothing can be seen, and the dust-blinded horses strive continually to turn from the blast. Once the Hungerford-Bourke coach was blown over and dragged across the driver, who, however, escaped without serious injury. During unusually heavy storms the team is turned tail to the wind, and a halt is made until the worst has blown over. Again, trees are blown across the road, and a way has to be picked slowly round through the timber.

Another danger which might at any time cause an accident is embodied in the simple-looking roley-poley, a huge white ball of burrs and grass. It is met with everywhere in the north-west, and rolls for miles across the plains, banking up against fences and filling up the cowals. These banks at night look like low hills, and the filled-up gutters resemble level strips of grassy ground. Horses are often frightened by the roley-poleys, which come spinning towards them, or suddenly roll across the track under their noses. They are weird-looking things in the moonlight, hundreds of them rolling along like scurrying sheep, bounding over the banked fences, and gambolling on again.

When it is mentioned that, besides drapery, spirits, and tobacco, such items as butter, fruit, bacon, hams, meat, vegetables, wool sheets, tents, tin dishes, and boots are sent through the parcels post, you can imagine what the non-postal matter is like. Every available inch of space is occupied, bags of chaff, buggy wheels, perambulators, and other bulky light stuff being piled on top to a height of several feet. Then there are the passengers, generally a mixed lot. Coming down, you might have a Chinaman beside you, and a couple of manacled prisoners, with a policeman on either side, on the opposite seat. And there is no room to stretch your legs or lean back; you are compelled to sit huddled in one position mile after mile, hour after hour. For this reason most people prefer the box seat. The inside is cooler on a hot day, warmer on a cold night, and drier in wet weather ; but you are cramped, and there is bound to be some old party alongside who can't keep awake, and who persists in making a pillow of his companion and snoring into his ear, or who bumps him heavily with every roll of the coach.

It is a genuine pleasure to see the lights of a town suddenly blaze out from the crest of a distant hill. In the early morning the place looks asleep, and during the day it has the dull sameness of many other towns ; but in the early night, when lights stream from everywhere, a little town looks big.

The coach often travels through miles of burning bush, enveloped in smoke and cinders, and running a hot race with long lines of flames that are closing in on the road. On the Glen Wills line, in Victoria, in February, 1905, the mail-coach and contents were destroyed, and three horses and a swagman—who had been picked up two miles back—were burnt to death. The coach had been traversing a cutting on the side of a hill, on which a fire was burning, when the wind sprang up suddenly and the flames leaped over the road in a broad sheet and completely enveloped it. The driver, who was knocked overboard and severely injured, escaped by crawling into Lightning Creek.

In February, 1902, while the mail-coach was travelling betwen Albury and Howlong, a goanna suddenly ran up the legs of one of the horses and perched on its back. The team became wildly excited, bolted, and smashed the vehicle against a tree. The goanna was about the only thing concerned that escaped injury.

Probably the worst disaster in the annals of backblocks coaching was that which overtook the Powell's Creek and Anthony's Lagoon (Northern Territory) mail, when the driver, passengers, and horses perished on a dry stage for want of water.

On the roads trending west from Bourke and north from Broken Hill it often happens in mid-summer that horses drop dead in harness from the excessive heat, and the driver, if unable to proceed with his weakened team, rides off to the nearest squattage or to the next mail change for fresh horses, while the passengers guard the coach and mails, and beguile the time the best way they can. While coming into Tibooburra one night a horse dropped from exhaustion, and the coach was pulled on to it before the team could be stopped. The coo-ees of the driver attracted a dozen of us to the scene, and after lifting the coach off the prostrate animal, and disentangling the others from the broken pole, we took hold fore and aft and rolled her on to the post-office. This, however, might be considered a good finish, when compared with the experience of a North Queensland mailman, who, when his horses caved in forty miles from Winton, carried the mailbags the rest of the way on his back, the journey occupying him two days.

These are some of the experiences of coaching in the tame times of the present. They were more exhilarating in the pioneering days of Cobb & Co., when the intrepid whips had to run the gauntlet of armed bushrangers, and often submit to being lined up with their passengers by the roadside while the coach was being ransacked. One of the famous whips of those days was Edward Devine, commonly known as Cabbage-tree Ned. From 1853 (when he was only seventeen) to 1862 Ned drove a six-in-hand between Geelong and Ballarat. During the first two years his wage was £16 a week, and his tips from lucky diggers, for whom he conveyed gold to the banks, averaged even more than that. The roads at the time were frequented by Captain Melville, Black Douglass, and other bushrangers. Ned had many narrow escapes, and on one occasion his coach was stuck up and his passengers robbed of £800 by the notorious Ned Jordan, afterwards hanged for the murder of Squatter Rutherford. Devine got his sobriquet from the fact that he usually sported a wide-brimmed cabbage-tree hat, made in Parramatta for the London International Exhibition held in 1851, and subsequently presented to him. It was a conspicuous part of his dress for 50 years.

H..P. ('DUKE') TRITTON

'A Close Friend of Johnny Vane'

From Time Means Tucker *(Sydney, 1964). The setting is outback New South Wales; the time: early 1900s.*

The driver of the mail coach, Gulargambone to Baradine, got sick and I took the job for a couple of weeks. The coach was one of the famous Cobb & Co. coaches. Probably over 20 years old, it was still in wonderful condition. Leather springs known as 'thoroughbraces' were still used. It used to sway and roll like a boat in a rough sea and I should imagine the passengers would get seasick on a long journey. The original cushions were in good order and 12 people would be seated comfortably. I had never driven four horses before but they knew their job and I had no trouble with them.

I picked up the mail at Gular at three in the afternoon and came back to Box Ridge, stayed the night, left for Baradine at eight, dropping mail at about 20 roadside mail boxes, changed horses at Goorianawa, then on to Bugaldi and Baradine, reaching there around four. The trip was just 70 miles. I did the round trip twice a week and found it somewhat boring unless I had passengers to yarn away the time. It might have been more interesting had there been a few bushrangers about. It would have been something to talk about in my old age.

Dick Knight, the regular driver, was close to 70. Born in Bathurst, N.S.W, he had driven mail coaches for most of his life. He had driven for Cobb & Co. on various runs for many years and know most of the bushrangers well, and was a close friend of Johnny Vane, one of the last of Ben Hall's gang. Johnny Vane had died in Bathurst the previous year (1906). It was Dick who told me the story of Jack Skillicorn, who had bet £100 that he would ride to Sydney from Bathurst on the one horse, between sunrise and sunset, in the one day. He completed the ride with time to spare, but the chaps who had followed him, with several changes of horses, refused to pay, because on several occasions he had dismounted for some reason or other, and before remounting had led the horse a few yards. Therefore, they argued, he had not ridden the horse *all* the way to Sydney. 'A dirty point,' Dick remarked. 'They saved their money, but for many years they were the most unpopular men in Bathurst.'

W. E. ('BILL') HARNEY

The Second Class Pushed

From North of 23 °: *Ramblings in Northern Australia (Sydney, 1946).*
Harney (1895–1962), drover, cattleman, patrol officer, soldier, wanderer,
writer, here tells of life in outback Queensland at the turn of the century.

———————————

Reaching Charleville I found work in a pub, washing dishes and
helping the housemaids, at 15 shillings a week and keep, but not
for long. A drover going north gave me a lift. I mustered his
horses in the morning and drove them behind his 'cook cart' all
day. I was grateful to him for the lift, but I worked my passage all
the way to Longreach on the Thomson River, where I camped on
the creek.

As my money was low, I attempted to walk the distance to
Winton, 128 miles away but gave up the venture through
loneliness and fear of the road, and paid my fare, 30 shillings, for
a ride in Cobb & Co.'s coach.

As we swung along in the rocking 'throughbrace' over those
rolling downs and through gidyea scrub, I read a book I had
picked up in an old camp. It was a tattered Shakespeare. I
staggered mentally through 'Othello' and read of the Moor
describing his travels to the father of Desdemona.

'Her father loved me, oft invited me, still questioned me the
story of my life——'

As I read away, the tender parts would bring tears to my eyes,
so that I would become ashamed of the other passsenger seeing
the tears, and wondering why I sorrowed.

I carried that book for years, until I earned enough money to
buy another. It was my wandering friend.

There was only one fare and one class when you travelled by Cobb & Co.; at least that is what I thought, as we all were together, until a chap told me there was a first and a second class. All rode together till the coach was bogged; then the second class pushed the coach, while the first class walked behind. God help the second class in a good rain, as the blacksoil plains were wide. Even the first class would have tough going, as the sticky mud would pile onto your boots, becoming larger with each step, until you became as weary as a prisoner with ball-and-chain on his legs. To remove the mud you would kick out violently, and often the boot itself would fly into the air, and leave you standing helplessly on one foot—or I should say on a ball of mud,—crying out for help.

Tale of the Old Coast Road

From Selected Poems of Marie E. J. Pitt *(Melbourne, 1944). Mrs Pitt, a Gippslander by birth, lived in the wild north-west of Tasmania for some twelve years following her marriage in 1893. Her literary life began during this period; and the strong influence of the region—its people and traditions—is reflected in several of her finest poems and ballads, including 'Tale of the Old Coast Road'.*

The big road-cars come flashing through like shuttles, south and
    north,
By Bishopsbourne to Launceston, by Sassafras to Forth,
And watching, in a waking dream, I hear the murmur grow,
The music of the Coast Road stream of fifty years ago;
The hillsides answer wheel and whip, wild echoes swell and fail,
As heavy o'er the blacksoil dip she comes, the Royal Mail—
I hear a loafing wheeler snort, the toiling leaders strain,
'From Table Cape by Devonport for the town of Deloraine'.

*   *   *

And this the tale they told to me when the children were abed,
And on the broad hearth merrily the little flames ran red,
How in the old south room he lay and drove his coach and four
As once he drove it everyday, as he would drive no more.
They tied the reins to his bed-foot, and in a land of dream
He raced his horses neck and neck against a phantom team;

133

Four blacks behind a leader pale as the white moon at the
    wane,
A coach without a passenger for the town of Deloraine.
Upon the big white leader's back a muffled horseman rode,
His head was down, his rein was slack, all loosely he bestrode;
No word of answering cheer he spake unto the sick man's hail,
Nor dallied he with whip or brake beside the Royal Mail;
What hot-head dared so rash a test? But woe the day or weal,
The old man's fighting soul confessed a foeman worth his steel,
And fiercely girt him for the fight while in life's silver chain
Death wove his dusky strand that night on the road to Deloraine.

And now he flogs them up the pinch black reared against the
    stars,
And feels her lifting inch by inch to creaking swingle bars;
And now across the stiff red loam he nurses them by fits,
Or feels them as the whip cuts home hang heavy on the bits.
But still the four black steeds come on behind their leader grey,
They fell behind him at the Don, they chased him thro'Torquay;
And starting from a broken sleep he takes the lead again
And swings them 'cross Rubicon for the town of Deloraine.

The wan moon hid a wistful face behind a granite crest,
Orion, Taurus, Pleiades, sank seaward down the west;
The sick man drowsed and drifted far from earth and human
    cares,
And paled the startled watchers at a footfall on the stairs;
A young wind whimpered at the pane of griefs that never slept,
And wild and white across the plain the keening plovers swept,
But in his sleep the dreamer smiled, belike he drove again
From Table Cape by Devonport for the town of Deloraine.

Upon the hearth the leaping red had dwindled ashen grey,
The nurse was nodding by the bed, and eastward broke the day.
All sudden stirred he, and his eyes strained backward thro' the
    gloom,

'They're here; they'll block us on the bridge; make room, I say,
    make room!
What dam foaled yon white-livered brute that gallops in the
    lead?
Who rides there? Answer, or I shoot! His voice shrilled like a reed.
'The bridge! The bridge!' His sobbing breath rose to a shout of
    pain—
'The bridge is down!—'tis us or Death to-night for Deloraine!'

'Get over! Up! Get up, my lads! So . . . . h-steady . . . . pull
    away;
We've left them at the Rubicon, the rest is only play.'
But still beside him in his dream the big black horses came,
And still he flayed his sweating team, blind, desperate, but game.
'Pull off!' his voice was harsh and high. 'Back, madman,
    back! . . . . too late!
The wheel's gone; God! the mail! . . . . then strong, exultant and
    elate
His voice rang in defiant cheer high over Death's domain—
'She lifts! . . . . She's free! . . . . What ho! the lights!—the lights
    of Deloraine.'

BILL WANNAN

Mick Dougherty and the Kangaroo

The material for this item, and the one that follows, have been taken from a booklet published by the Harrietville Historical Society, Victoria, on the occasion of the unveiling of a plaque to honour the memory of Mick Dougherty (pronounced Dockerty), coachdriver, in 1962. The booklet opens with these words:

MICK DOUGHERTY
Much Loved Coachdriver and Raconteur
of Bush Stories
1854–1923

Today, Sunday, December 30th, 1962, we stand beside this rippling river, in the shade of the Mountains loved by that famous old Coachdriver, Mick Dougherty, to do him honor.

On the Seat of Iron stained Quartz, facing the road traversed by the Coaches in the Coaching Days, the beautiful copper Plaque, embellished in enamel with a Coach and four grey horses, bears this inscription:
'TO THE MEMORY OF A WAY OF LIFE NOW GONE.'
'A TRIBUTE TO MICK DOUGHERTY AND HIS FELLOW DRIVERS.'

Mick Dougherty never drove a coach for Cobb & Co., as many people believe. Most of his driving was done for the coach line founded by Hiram A. Crawford,—Crawford & Co., later Crawford & Connelly. This line served the rugged north-east of Victoria, with headquarters behind Tanswell's Hotel in Beechworth.

Mick was widely hailed in his lifetime as 'the greatest liar in

Australia', but he bestowed that honour on a clergyman, Mr Rivett, following a tall-tale telling session between them. 'I never met such a liar as Mr Rivett,' said Mick, admitting defeat.

Here's a variant of the most popular yarn ever attributed to Mick. It concerns an occasion when an elderly lady, just out from England, was Buffalo bound on the box seat of Mick Dougherty's coach. They'd travelled a few miles when the lady turned to Mick and said, 'My relatives have warned me that you're the biggest liar in Australia, so I'm not going to believe one word you tell me.'

Dougherty made out that he was most insulted. However, after the coach had been on the road for some time he started to tell a remarkable story of a kangaroo which he claimed he'd trained to meet the coach. He'd throw a mailbag to the 'roo, he said, and the animal would then open the bag, sort out the letters and parcels, and deliver them to the settlers in the nearby areas.

'Mr Dougherty, you don't expect me to believe that!' the old lady exclaimed.

However, a few metres further on the coach came to a sharp bend in the bush track. Standing right in the middle of the road was an old man kangaroo.

Mick Dougherty didn't hesitate. Cracking his whip, he shouted, 'Nothing today, Jack!'

The kangaroo turned and made off into the scrub, much to the old lady's surprise.

Another of Mick's stories is recorded by Alan D. Mickle in his book, *Many a Mickle*. It told of 'the intense cold up on Mount Buffalo in the wintertime. He would say that some men were camped there and one of them one night tried to blow out the candle, but could not move the flame. Then he discovered that it was frozen and he had to hold it over the camp fire until the light had melted enough for him to blow it out.'

DONALD McDONALD

Some Recollections of Mick Dougherty

From a booklet published by the Harrietville Historical Society, Victoria, on the occasion of the unveiling of a plaque in honour of Mick Dougherty in 1962.

'Pardon me, are you Mr Dougherty?'

'I'm not, Sir. I'm Mick Dougherty.'

'Ah, that's lucky, because it was really Mick Dougherty I wanted to meet.'

And from that first characteristic introduction upon the high plateau which had been his excelsior for the great part of his life, acquaintance with Mick Dougherty rapidly improved. I had heard much of him long before I met him, but the personality visualised was quite unlike the man. He was not the old type of driver who in the beginning sat upon the box seat for 'Cobb & Co.'—and I had some knowledge of them almost from infancy, for my father was one of that group of Scottish Canadians, who came here with A. W. Robertson and who were generally known as 'the Yankees', though most of them were Glengarry men from that area of Ontario about which 'Ralph Connor' has written so much. They were for the most part big men who wore their beards pointed, in the later sailor style, and who perpetually, it seemed to me, carried a cigar in the left corner of the mouth, the only place one could smoke it and keep both hands free for the business of driving. These were mostly plainsmen on the long routes, Swan Hill, Deniliquin, Warrnambool, and I have heard my father say, that on occasions when the Murray met its own loops, like the Wakool and Edwards, over the flooded plains, he has driven the big Bendigo coach from Moama to Deniliquin without ever getting out of water.

Mick Dougherty's driving. . . was almost always amongst the hills, and he lived much upon the edge of something that with the least miscalculation might make a nasty mess. He was under average height, thick-set, with a round, good-humoured Irish face, and a pair of pleasant blue eyes which beamed perpetual good nature. Those eyes, unlike any others I have seen, were the windows through which you looked into the unusually fine nature of this most likeable man.

Before meeting him I heard much of the manner in which he was accustomed to enliven the way, entertain his passengers with quaint story, quip and catch; but that was not all—nothing like all—of Mick Dougherty when you came to know him. His best stories were often told with deliberately good-hearted intent, reserved for those nasty places on the battlement of the Buffalo where it was not good, not comfortable or reassuring, to look down and let your imagination get away with you. Mick Dougherty was too kind a man to see a woman or a nervous man suffer, so he kept them distracted in those perilous places where the road as you look up to it, so often suggests a broad pencil mark across the cliff faces, and the feature of the Buffalo road when you first look at it is, that above all other places you have known, it seems as a road quite impassable.

Clever as he was in handling his team of coach horses, he was equally clever in guiding the conversation just where he wanted it for someone to ask the inevitable question. And there was one little touch in his story telling which revealed the real genial human nature of the man. Mick Dougherty was never the hero of his own anecdotes and reminiscences, always the butt or victim of them, and you felt perfectly sure that he often deliberately put himself in an inglorious position where his own mental alertness would never have landed him.

In the Kelly days [the late 1870s] there were exciting times for coach-drivers in that region, if only in apprehension of the thing that never occurred, because back nearly as far as Ned Kelly's time robbing coaches was never really worth while. 'And they'll tell ye proudly up there,' Mick remarked to me once, 'that Ned Kelly never robbed the poor. Isn't it foolish for to talk that way. Why would anyone rob the poor when he would get nothing for his pains? They would not hurt the man they robbed, and they would not profit themselves. When thim lads went to stick-up, it wasn't playactin'.'

By consent of both sides, and as a matter of common fair play, Mick Dougherty was a neutral. Some of the Police, Sergeant Steele, with the clean-cut aquiline profile, and Strahan, of the bulldog breed, a rare stickler on criminal tracks, both put it to Mick that he should see nothing, and tell nothing, either way, and he kept rigidly to that compact. 'You might put us in the way of catching the Kellys,' Steele said, 'but if anything went wrong, what would your life be worth?' So Mick Dougherty kept his own counsel, said nothing and suffered nothing. He was too shrewd for heroics.

Many a night a man rode up suddenly alongside the off fore wheel with a request for a parcel marked for delivery elsewhere. Sometimes it was tea, or sugar, or oatmeal, much more frequently it was whisky, or a demijohn of beer with a vinegar label on it. The man who took it with an almost whispered 'Goodnight, Mick,' rode off into the trees again, and Mick Dougherty, thinking much, said nothing.

I once talked to Mick about the Kellys, and the impression, as I recall it, was that Ned at least looked a man, and two of his gang decidedly did not. The long beard gave him a touch of dignity. The worst feature of his face was that the eyebrows approached each other too closely, too heavily, or as Mick Dougherty put it, 'There was a bit o' the wild dog in the corners of his eyes. And Dan, well a bad wretch that, hatchet faced and yellow. . . If Dan Kelly was given his way, the lot of them would ha' been shot like Morgan, from behind a tree, long before the police got 'em. And Steve Hart—only a weed—a bit o' a horse jockey, nothing else.'

It seemed a drop in rank, a loss of caste, when a King of the

Road, the daring Alpine driver, was given charge of donkeys at the end of his days. I talked about it just a year ago with Mick Dougherty on a Sunday morning as we sat on the sunny side of a granite tor on the top of Buffalo. 'Yes, it's a funny thing, isn't it,' he said, 'that a man like me, that's handled horses, and driven horses, and loved horses, too, should be handling donkeys for his living at the last. But the strangest thing of all is that I find myself with a greater likin' for them things than for the finest horse I ever drove—and I've had good ones on these roads, greys with the Snowden mark on them . . . horses with the Panic blood through Terror, that were class enough to win a steeplechase— and I'm fonder of these things than I ever was of them. How do you explain it all? Is it the long ears, or the way the people laugh at them, or the patient look o' them that makes you pity them first, and love 'em afterwards? They have great jokes about them up here, but sometimes I think that if they were good enough for the Redeemer of the world, they ought to be good enough for almost anybody. Look at that lad over there now, one ear nether, and the other over. Could you help liking them?'

Mick Dougherty was of all things observant. Riding on the box with him you realised in every chance observation his wide knowledge of things that count in the Mountains. Perhaps it was a herd of scraggy store cattle coming down out of the snows. Mick summed them up with a curt, 'Look at 'em. All blacks, blues and brindles!' If you described them for half an hour, you would not say more in condemnation than those few words which mean so much to a cattle man.

A man of parts, with an individuality which is somewhat rare, one to be respected when living, and lovingly remembered after death. Something has gone from the Buffalo, and the Buffalo road, that can never come back to it, and we are poorer for the loss however easy the motor man may make it for us in the years to come.

'My Team of Greys'

From the Benalla Standard, *Victoria (19 February, 1948)*.

In October 1934 two great historic events coincided—the Centenary Air Race from London to Melbourne, and a conference of drivers of Cobb & Co.'s famous old horse coaches.

Two intrepid British airmen made the cross-world flight in a little over two days. As the aerial speedsters zoomed over Melbourne somebody tried to electrify the coachies' confab by shouting to them: 'Scott and Black are arriving.'

'Yes, yes,' said a patriarchal driver, but turning to his comrade he continued—'as I was saying, my team of greys. . .'

'Greys be blowed!' retorted another earnest veteran; 'my team of bays could eat them alive before breakfast on any road in any weather, and. . .'

And so the weighty argument ran for hours. Airmen might come and go, circle the globe, skim through the stars, but to these champions of the old coach roads, the rival matter of bays and greys was a matter supreme.

The first reunion of Cobb coachmen was held in the Melbourne Exhibition Building on 5 May, 1925. Most of the men were in their seventies, some in their eighties and nineties. The ages of five of the elders aggregated 437 years. How they talked and toasted the old days! And their talk was priceless, for they handled the ribbons, cracked the whip and sounded the merry horn from the days of the hectic gold rushes onward.

Through the wild bush country, from the rich diggings of Ballarat and Bendigo, their flashing six-in-hands had brought untold treasure to the growing city of Melbourne. Records attest that at one time and another no less than 36 Cobb coaches were bailed up by bushrangers.

ERNIE RICHARDS

The Old Coaching Days

During the year 1963 the firm of Cobb & Co., which operates a modern fleet of motorised transports in the interior of Queensland, with headquarters at Toowoomba, participated in a unique event to help in publicising the work of the Royal Flying Doctor Service. This was an epic drive by one of the old Cobb coaches from Port Douglas, in far northern Queensland, to Melbourne–a journey of nearly 3,000 miles. (The longest previous coach run, by Wells Fargo in the United States, was 2,200 miles.) On this occasion, one of the drivers was Ernie Richards, who, I think I'm right in saying, was the youngest surviving of the original drivers of the Royal Mail coaches of Cobb and Co.

The verse which follows was written by Ernie and published in broadsheet form in 1959. A copy was sent to me by Mr Len Williams of Goondiwindi, (Qld) in July 1963 with the comment: 'Would be pleased if you would print the poetry as it should be of interest everywhere.'

On our Long Journey out into the Great Far West of Queens-
    sland, we GO,—
Travelling by the Thoro'brace Coaches and the Hundreds of
    Horses of COBB & Co.,—
Starting off at Break of Day, and in Wet Weather arriving at any
    hour, of the NIGHT,—
Over Rough Roads and Bush Tracks, Passengers to their Seats
    often had to hang TIGHT,—
Travelling all thru' the Hot and Dusty Day, list'ning to the
    Coach Wheels' SONG,—
Passing Wild Birds, Chirping along the Rivers·and the Creeks
    and by the Old BILLABONG,—

By Day the Laughing Jackass, the Stormbird, the Old Crew, and
the LARK,—

The Curlew and the Mopoke, as the Coaches rumbled along in
the DARK,—

With Thunder and Lightning, and a Storm in the West, rising
FAST,—

Then Battling thru' Rain and Mud, we arrived at the Night
Stage at LAST,—

Coach Passengers stayed Overnight, at the Old Slab Built,
Wayside PUB,—

Where its Fat Lamps could be seen Flaring, through the Dark
and Thick SCRUB,—

Along the Banks of the Warrego, Barcoo, Paroo, The Cooper,
Flinders and the DIAMANTINA,—

Coach Passengers spent many a Night, Dancing to an Old Fiddle
or a CONCERTINA,—

Before Daybreak, the Teamster's Big Bullfrog, Condamine
BELL,—

Could be heard, Ringing, Five Miles away, or'e Hill and
DELL,—

Churches, Clergymen, and Doctors, in the Great Outback, were
Far and FEW,—

God's Blessings always on the Old Hands, who could cook a
Damper in the Ashes, and out of Nothing make a good Hot
STEW,—

The Drover on his Night Horse, riding round his Mob of Cattle,
on Late WATCH,—

Never forgot to ask the Coachdriver, to have a Pot of Black Tea, a
Rum, or a SCOTCH,—

After receiving his Mail and Parcels with a Smile both Cheery
and BRIGHT,—

Wished the Driver the 'Best of Luck', as he drove on thru' a
terrifying Storm in the Black OF NIGHT,—

Across shifting Sand Hills, Dry Rivers, and Hot Scorching
PLAINS,—

The Mails and Rations were carried by Coaches, Pack Horse,

and Long CAMEL TRAINS,—

When heading across the Far Western Plains, which were so
LARGE,—

Explorers and many Others perished when what they thought to
be Water was only a MIRAGE,—

Many a Man broke, humped his Swag, camped on the bank of a
CREEK,—

With work hard to find, tramped the Back Country, Week after
WEEK,—

Travelling along the many lonely miles of densely timbered Bush
TRACKS,—

Coachdrivers had to contend with Bushrangers, and the old
Pioneers with Wild BLACKS,—

No one ever grumbled when they travelled in the old Coaching
DAYS,—

'All Aboard' on Cobb's Coaches, with their teams of Greys,
Browns, Chestnuts and BAYS,—

Cobb's Coaches pioneered the transport of passengers in the days
of YORE,—

The last Cobb & Co. Coach ran in Queensland from Surat to
Yeulba, in the year 1924,—

On our Advance Australia Emblem, we have the Rising Sun, the
Emu, and the KANGAROO,—

To remind us always of those Transport Pioneers, who blazed the
Trails THRU',—

And when the early history of road transport of this Great
CONTINENT,—

Is written, from the stories of hardships of those who lived in a
Bark Hut or a TENT,—

With the Sun shining by day, and the Moon and the Stars that
kept the Nights AGLO',—

List'ning for the Bugle Call, and the Whipcrack, and Watching
for the Royal Mail Coaches of COBB & CO.